Advanced Praise for *Beyond the Offering Plate*

"I, like many of my clergy friends, tend to focus all my stewardship efforts on either time/talent or treasure. Depending on the year, I tip to one side or the other. Adam Copeland's project, *Beyond the Offering Plate*, offers an extremely helpful corrective. Copeland, along with all the contributors, continuously holds out a much more holistic understanding of stewardship than my more programmatic approach to the church budget. I am thankful for the challenges embedded in the pages of this book, as well as the encouragement and inspiration it offers!"

—Shannon J. Kershner, pastor, Fourth
Presbyterian Church, Chicago

"*Beyond the Offering Plate* will expand your understanding of stewardship. Too often the word is used to describe only what a congregation does to get its bills paid. Stewardship is far too rich to be so limited. Thought-provoking writers and excellent discussion questions make the book especially suited for group study. I strongly recommend it to your congregation's leaders."

—Charles R. Lane, pastor, Lord of Life Lutheran
Church; coauthor of *Embracing Stewardship*;
and author of *Ask, Thank, Tell*

"A refreshing look at a more holistic approach to stewardship in daily life and congregations. This collection can stimulate thinking and conversation about the evolving role of stewardship in a changing church."

—Keith A. Mundy, program director,
Office of Stewardship, Evangelical Lutheran
Church in America

"In *Beyond the Offering Plate: A Holistic Approach to Stewardship*, one writer notes that 'Stewardship is not so much a series of actions as an orientation . . . nurture the gracious gifts of Gc   s mindset is a theme throug   ardship

D1473068

educators, and laypersons alike will appreciate these diverse and thoughtful essays, study questions, and sermon ideas. Prepare to dive deeply into new and rediscovered aspects of this Christian spiritual discipline."

—Marcia Shetler, executive director/CEO, Ecumenical Stewardship Center

"Expanding far beyond the limits most of us put around stewardship, this book takes a whole person and whole community approach to focusing our lives around God's priorities. It is nothing less than a call to reimagine stewardship of the church for the twenty-first century and stretch our thinking about how to lead."

—Jeff Thiemann, president/CEO, Portico Benefit Services, a ministry of the Evangelical Lutheran Church in America

Beyond the Offering Plate

Beyond the Offering Plate

A Holistic Approach to Stewardship

Adam J. Copeland, editor

WESTMINSTER
JOHN KNOX PRESS
LOUISVILLE · KENTUCKY

First edition
Published by Westminster John Knox Press
Louisville, Kentucky

17 18 19 20 21 22 23 24 25 26—10 9 8 7 6 5 4 3 2 1

Excerpts from Carolyn Browning Helsel, "Sermon on Philippians 2" (unpublished sermon, Austin Presbyterian Theological Seminary, April 25, 2016), are used by permission. All rights reserved. Excerpts from Kris Tostengard Michel, "What Are You Worth: Proverbs 22:9" (unpublished sermon, Bethlehem Lutheran Church, October 4, 2015), are used by permission. All rights reserved.

Scripture quotations are from the New Revised Standard Version of the Bible, copyright © 1989 by the Division of Christian Education of the National Council of the Churches of Christ in the U.S.A., and are used by permission.

Book design by Sharon Adams
Cover design by Mark Abrams

Library of Congress Cataloging-in-Publication Data

Names: Copeland, Adam J., 1983- editor.
Title: Beyond the offering plate : a holistic approach to stewardship / Adam J. Copeland, editor.
Description: Louisville, KY : Westminster John Knox Press, [2017] | Identifiers: LCCN 2017005497 (print) | LCCN 2017021346 (ebook) | ISBN 9781611648119 (ebk.) | ISBN 9780664262358 (pbk. : alk. paper)
Subjects: LCSH: Christian stewardship. | Christian giving.
Classification: LCC BV772 (ebook) | LCC BV772 .B49 2017 (print) | DDC 248/.6--dc23
LC record available at https://lccn.loc.gov/2017005497

∞ The paper used in this publication meets the minimum requirements of the American National Standard for Information Sciences—Permanence of Paper for Printed Library Materials, ANSI Z39.48-1992.

Most Westminster John Knox Press books are available at special quantity discounts when purchased in bulk by corporations, organizations, and special-interest groups. For more information, please e-mail SpecialSales@wjkbooks.com.

Contents

Foreword

In the congregations and seminaries I have known, talk about stewardship relies on a set of affirmations with which theologians, church leaders, and congregants typically agree. Stewardship is not just about money. Everything that we are and have belongs to God, not to us. Returning to God some of the gifts we have received is a crucial expression of our faith. Together as church, we know these things to be true.

Often, however, these and similar affirmations seem to float above the actual life of the church. They can remain abstract and distant from the real concerns of cash-strapped Christian congregations and their costly mission of love and service to a hurting world. Come Stewardship Sunday, anxiety is in the air, in spite of the upbeat theme and encouraging talks prepared by each year's lay leaders. In the pews, there are questions. How much should I give? How much are they giving? Will we as a body raise enough to meet local and mission needs? Okay, this is not just about money, and everything is God's, and giving expresses my faith. But still.

Adam Copeland has gathered a group of thoughtful authors who bring stewardship down to earth and into play in many domains of everyday life. In their chapters, an abstract theology of gifts and giving, which too often remains at the level of ideals, becomes an engaged practical theology that takes shape within the often messy lives of persons and communities. When the insights in this book begin to reshape church leaders' understanding of stewardship and to take hold in congregations, there will still be questions in the pews, one of which will still be "how much money should I give?" Beyond this, however, Christians will also need to ask: "How is the work I do part of my stewardship of God's gifts?" "How does caring for beautiful, vulnerable human bodies—my own and those of others—express my trust in God's love for this material, broken, and promise-filled world?" "How am I, and how are we as a congregation, located within this world's hierarchies of privilege, and how shall we steward the opportunities of this location on behalf of justice and peace?" Indeed, the questions we need to ask will abound, depending not on distant ideals but on the actual contours of faithful living in each place of ministry and life.

In fact, the people in our congregations already steward God's gifts across many domains of living—including in their relationships with others, their work, and, yes, their finances. Yet many long to do so more faithfully, and all need language well suited to exploring the questions at stake in the wise use of all that God has made and entrusted, temporarily, to our care. Today's Christians urgently need to have sustained conversations about stewarding their gifts—all their gifts—in response to God's grace. This book's expansion of the reach and meaning of talk about stewardship will greatly enrich these conversations.

—Dorothy C. Bass,
director emerita of the Valparaiso Project
on the Education and Formation of People in Faith

Acknowledgments

This book would not have been possible without a host of able co-creators to whom I am so very grateful. To each and every writer, thank you for sharing your wisdom and expanding our imaginations. Their insightful contributions are a true gift to the church and academy, and I am exceptionally grateful for the authors' support of this project. As the reader will find, the writers featured in these pages offer an enormous wealth of life experience, theological expertise, and abiding love for God. Moreover, that they stewarded their time to this project gives testament to their love and hope for God's church. Many thanks, as well, to my colleagues at Luther Seminary for inviting me to lead the Center for Stewardship Leaders and for providing me space and support to live into new expressions of stewardship. My chapter on the stewardship of technology was strengthened by my colleague Terri Elton's attentive and kindhearted comments. Thanks also to René Mehlberg for her template wrangling, editorial support, and for kindly suffering my deluge of emails to her. Further thanks to Alexandra Benson for sharing her practical wisdom in the revision process. To the generous donors who endowed the Center for Stewardship Leaders, the church is more vital, generous, and faithful because of your commitment to educating future stewardship leaders. Many sincere thanks to my editor at Westminster John Knox Press, David Maxwell, for expertly guiding this manuscript to publication. Finally, for the loving support of my wife, Megan, whose partnership makes my life whole, I express my deepest thanks. I dedicate this book to my parents who, in their loving wisdom, quiet kindness, and faithful witness, have modeled and taught me—and so many others—how to steward God's gifts.

Introduction

I'm sorry. Those words often accompany stewardship conversations in many congregations today. Pastors explain, "I'm sorry for the awkwardness of needing to raise my own salary, but it's again time for our annual stewardship campaign." Treasurers announce, "I'm sorry to share that we are behind on our budget." Members say—or, at least, think—"I'm sorry we have to talk about money, and in church of all places!" I have a few theories concerning the roots of these rampant stewardship apologies.

First, let's admit upfront that talking about money in public makes many of us uncomfortable. It's a great irony that, in a country in which conspicuous consumption reigns and pursuit of the almighty dollar spurs our work and (supposed) worth, we actually prefer to avoid money conversations in public. Think I'm wrong? With how many people have you discussed your annual salary? How many friends know how much you gave to charity last year? What members of your family know your true financial condition? Since we so rarely address money in public settings, it makes sense that money talk in church makes many of us a bit uncomfortable. And so church leaders, out of their desire not to ruffle too many feathers, approach stewardship apologetically.

Second, behind that hesitancy to discuss money in public is a related discomfort with our relationship to money. Money is essential to our economic system. Jesus talked about it often. And yet, we don't quite know what to do with it, how to approach it, or what to feel about it. Many pastors I work with hesitate when asked to describe a theology of money. Remarkably few have had the opportunity to ponder money with any theological sophistication. Given this reality among many church leaders, it's no wonder that congregation members may sense uneasiness on the part of clergy when money comes up in church. Many pastors themselves feel anxious, out of their depth, or even shame around the topic of money.

Third, and perhaps most important, I believe our apologetic approach to financial stewardship has to do with a deep longing for more (substance, not money). We know that speaking about money once a year during the annual campaign reflects too thin a theology. The typical approach to stewardship in congregations leaves us unsatisfied. Talking about stewardship once a year, and only in terms of financial stewardship, is like sitting down to a four-course meal, but leaving after only a few bites of the appetizer. Even if those few bites are delicious, a hunger remains.

For these reasons and more, the church needs stronger, wiser, and more creative ministry that addresses financial stewardship. I am very fortunate to regularly teach a course at Luther Seminary titled, "Money and the Mission of the Church." Though the course is offered as an elective, it is usually oversubscribed. Students know that Christian public leadership today requires savvy with financial stewardship, so they enroll in large numbers. While very few students discern a call to ordained ministry because of money, they appreciate the value of stewardship leadership. Even so, we end every semester with more questions than answers. It turns out that mastering financial stewardship is a life's work and fails to fit on a single semester's syllabus.

Most of those who preach or talk about stewardship focus only on money-related aspects of the term. Too often, I have counted myself among these ranks, introducing a presentation with a statement along these lines: "Of course, stewardship is much broader than money. Stewardship is holistic, and importantly expands beyond finances. But since my time is limited today, I'm going to focus on the topic of money and financial stewardship." The financial aspect of stewardship is plenty complicated by itself, so it's difficult to range beyond money, especially when congregations seek to meet—or raise—their budgets. This book finally takes up the invitation to broaden the stewardship conversation beyond money alone.

Just as there is a hunger in congregations for richer, more honest conversation related to money, there exists also a large opening for claiming the fullness of stewardship. A friend recently alerted me to an acquaintance's Facebook status. Clicking over, I found the following in her Facebook status:

> Every once in a while, I discover that a word has kind of been hijacked. This happened to the words "orthodox" and "evangelical." When people hear either word, they have a narrow, specific meaning that pops to mind, and that meaning usually doesn't work for me. "Stewardship" has had the same fate.
>
> This grand word with sweeping implications for lives of living in communion with all creation, caring for the gifts God has given us . . . we have decided it really mostly applies to our money.
>
> What a total bummer.

A bummer indeed. This book exists to fill that void.

In Jody Shipka's groundbreaking book, *Toward a Composition Made Whole* (2011), she argues that the field of writing studies and composition had too long emphasized written text on a static page, when in fact meaning-making and writing have to do with varied visual, aural, and multimedia forms. I have created this book resting upon the assertion that the church's approach to stewardship, too, must be broadened. Sound financial stewardship is deepened by a holistic stewardship.

Given the financial realities in many congregations, some may worry that taking time away from discussions related to stewardship of money will distract from the important, needed money-focused stewardship study. I contend, however, that making the stewardship conversation whole in fact enriches, deepens, and supports financial stewardship. In solidarity with many stewardship authors, I agree that the goal of stewardship ministry is not ultimately raising the budget, nor even necessarily related to finances. Stewardship ministry, like all good practical theology, affirms our broad call to love God and neighbor. All too often, however, stewardship becomes aligned narrowly with fundraising. What good is an annual stewardship campaign that raises the budget but fails to build rich faith in Christ? If stewardship means only money, it means so little as to be nearly worthless.

Holistic stewardship thinking and communication, when engaged well, meets people in practical, longed-for ways. Indeed, my close friends and relations live holistic stewardship daily by stewarding old houses and mortgages; by nurturing the boat motor back to life each summer; by becoming aware of the privilege of their education, faith, and/or skin color; by keeping and repairing marriage covenants; by caring for their pets; by voting in elections; by supporting worthy institutions; by feeding their bodies; by speaking the truth in love; by raising their children; and so much more. This book might be seen as a way into financial stewardship. And I do hope it is that. The book is also intended, however, as an expansion.

Like a fugue by J. S. Bach that begins with a short theme, then blossoms into rich, textured variations on that theme, my conception of stewardship includes money in its melodic theme. But by expanding the theme, the whole composition is richer and more beautiful. The theme alone is perfectly serviceable, reasonably pleasing, but it blooms to become an even more beautiful whole when played in full.

Definitions of stewardship tend to emphasize this broader view. I understand stewardship to be a lived theology founded on the claim that all resources begin with and belong to God.

Practicing stewardship reshapes how Christians manage all resources including "our" money, materials, and relationships. Stewardship is a lived concept, most often resulting in sharing that surprises, compassion that complicates, and love that inspires.

In too many places, I have seen the derivation of the word *steward* mistaken, so I seek to correct the record here by drawing upon the ever-dependable *Oxford English Dictionary (OED)*. From the Old English word, *stigweard*, a steward was an official keeper of a house or some part of a house. The *OED* makes clear "there is no ground for the assumption that *stigweard* originally meant 'keeper of the pig-sties.'"[1] Though his formal title is Butler, the word's actual origin reminds me of the care with which Mr. Carson, the butler in the hit television show *Downton Abbey*, goes about his work. Carson has a keen sense of respect for the great old house itself, and for its traditions, standards, and stories. Though his life is intimately tied to the house, Carson is clear never to confuse it as his own. He works to steward that which is not his, yet is certainly his responsibility to manage.

Though we may learn from the past, today we find ourselves far from the times of Old English and sprawling abbeys. Yet we have so much to steward. In the pages that follow, wise writers take up the invitation to envision new ways of stewarding the concerns of the present. Since money is (rightfully) unavoidable when it comes to stewardship, this collection includes a splendid chapter by David King exploring a robust theology of money and finances, as well as an invitation to generosity. Otherwise, the pages that follow expand the notion of stewardship beyond the usual suspects, while also inviting alternative entry points to more common topics. For example, every chapter addresses realities related to stewardship of God's creation, including ourselves and our possessions, as well as our bodies, the institutions with which we associate, and the spaces we inhabit. I hope such an approach furthers exploration into the implications of holistic stewardship with the nonhuman members and elements of creation. Indeed, this collection serves as a sort of extended invitation to the church, asking the question: what happens when we explore new, more holistic conceptions regarding "stewardship of _____"? Any published collection faces limits of space and expertise, so I embrace and invite further extensions of the field, reworked questions, and other approaches to help make stewardship whole.

These chapters also implicate the tendency in some circles to personalize stewardship in a manner that makes stewardship overly individualistic. In congregations, invitations to financial giving often embrace appeals to self-interest and personal choice. When taken to the extreme, this approach can result in the myopic notion that (financial) stewardship is only "between me and God." Threaded through these pages rests a plea for a deep appreciation of the ways stewardship flourishes when understood as layered, interrelated, and interdependent. Whole stewardship concerns, not only how I manage my money, but how our financial system supports fair exchange of goods and services. Whole stewardship concerns, not only how I care for my body, but—by the nature of my embodied living with others—how I care for community and the bodies of my neighbors. Whole stewardship concerns, not only personal intellectual stimulation, but how I teach others, learn from others, and even what information is accessible to the public. Stewardship certainly calls for individual action, but such action must also be appreciative of the interdependent nature of life together.

It is my sincere hope that this book will become a resource for ministry of many sorts. To that end, several aids for readers are included. Reflection questions and ideas for application in congregations follow each chapter. A concluding chapter includes biblical texts and themes appropriate for preaching.

Adam J. Copeland
Summer 2016

1

Stewardship of Time

Clocks, Calendars, and Cathedrals

MARYANN McKIBBEN DANA

Amazon founder Jeff Bezos is helping build a 10,000-year clock. To be more specific, he's provided the land and some $42 million to make it happen. But it's not a solitary vanity project for the multi-billionaire—some 3,300 people have contributed money to help build the clock, through a foundation set up for that purpose. The organization is called Long Now, which is one of the more delightful names I've run across for a foundation.

It's an ironic project for Bezos, who made his fortune off promising us more and more stuff in less and less time. But even Bezos realizes that operating under such short time-frames takes a toll on our civilization and our planet. If we're going to survive as a species, we're going to need to look beyond the quick fix. "We humans have become so technologically sophisticated that in certain ways we're dangerous to ourselves," he told the *Wall Street Journal* in 2012. "It's going to be increasingly important over time for humanity to take a longer-term view of its future."[1]

How will Long Now ensure the clock works for 10,000 years? The clock will be powered by humans, with a backup solar option if we become extinct. It will be buried in a mountain for stability and safety. And the building materials will need to be durable enough to withstand the very passage of time the clock will measure.

Many people would look at a 10,000-year clock as a colossal waste of money. Why wasn't this money given to cancer research, for example? However, a 2013 *Business Insider* article chides our selective outrage: "America, you spend $633,000 per day on Candy Crush Saga," amounting to $56 million over a three-month period.[2]

It is a lot of money. But I can't bring myself to wring my hands over the waste at building a clock that will measure time for a hundred centuries. Instead, I lament the fact that the church isn't the one doing it.

Why don't we build great cathedrals anymore? I know, I know—the church of the future is agile and diverse and flexible. Many of us in the church have criticized our tendency to get too hung up on the big permanent structures—the buildings, the monuments to God—rather than on being the people sent. Cathedrals, and the way we cling to them and all their various trappings, are our problem. I get it. The Tower of Babel can too easily be decked out in stained glass and long-throw LCD projectors.

But a good cathedral, in addition to being a gorgeous sacred space, is also a profound statement about time—what will endure, what will last. Several years ago, I visited the *Sagrada Familia* cathedral in Barcelona, which had been under construction for some hundred years. I hear it's done now. Part of me is disappointed it's complete—something in me liked the idea of our never quite finishing something that's dedicated to the glory of God, whose steadfast love endures forever. I think about how many workers have poured their labor into that place, knowing they would not live to complete it. I imagine the multitudes of Barcelonans living their lives in the shadow of that cathedral—both the completed portions *and* the scaffolding covering areas of the cathedral they would not live to see completed.

There are sound financial reasons why we don't build cathedrals anymore. In an era of shrinking budgets and declining members, it's not good stewardship. But I wonder if there is a spiritual reason too. We're rightly busy caring for the flock, feeding the hungry in our communities, and other biblical imperatives. But do we also avoid grand projects spanning multiple generations out of an impoverished sense of eschatology and the new heaven and new earth God envisions for us and makes real through Christ? If we trust that we're really headed somewhere, that our God is infinite, isn't it worthwhile to start a project, even if we won't see it finished? Indeed, is there any other kind of gospel pursuit?

"The [reign] of God is at hand," Jesus preached, or alternately, "the [reign] of God is among you" (see Mark 1:15; Luke 17:21). As mainline Christians who like to get concrete things done, we are comfortable with a realized eschatology. We're good at it. Our job is to find where God is and join God there. We're less comfortable with an eschatology that points to the future—the far future. And that's a loss.

At any rate, the world seems to be moving too fast for cathedrals. We in the church are as captive as anyone to a culture of instant results. A cathedral takes patience, sacrifice, and a sense of delayed gratification.

Over the years I've spoken to a lot of individuals, groups, and congregations about how we live in time—whether we move with a savoring pace, or not; how we discern what is ours to do in a world crammed with options for our time. Many people are overwhelmed and stressed out, torn by family responsibilities, careers, information overload, and more; and such overwork takes its toll. Anxiety specialist Dr. Robert Leahy estimates that the average high-school student today carries as much anxiety as the average psychiatric patient in the 1950s.[3] Even those of us who are retired, who left paid work a long time ago, feel overwhelmed by the pace of change. "I'm not on Facebook, which means I can't keep up with what's going on with my grandkids" is a common lament. I noted in a sermon a few years ago that roughly 300 hours of video are uploaded to YouTube every minute. That statistic turns out to be wrong; it's 400 hours per minute, though by the time this book is published it will be even greater.[4] Obsolescence is in the air we breathe.

Amid all this dysfunction, stewardship of time feels like a tricky needle to thread.

At its worst, stewardship of time can devolve into a trumped-up term for self-improvement. We want to use our time well, and there are countless tools to help us manage our time and our lives. I rely on Evernote, a to-do list app, with alarms, reminders, and programs that will turn off the Internet at specified times so I can get work done without distraction. These tools allow me to quiet the noise and to offload the tasks I'm liable to forget so I don't have to worry about them. My mind is clearer for having a system in place. But I'm kidding myself if I think all these tools will guide me into a faithful, integrated life. They help with time management, but not stewardship of time.

It's absolutely essential, I believe, to be intentional about how we live our days—how much activity we're willing to pack into our lives; whether we are attentive to the people around us, or perpetually distracted by buzzes and dings and our own monkey-mind.

The tricky aspect of stewardship of time, as opposed to other aspects of our lives, is this: we never really know how much time we have. As a forty-four-year old, I know what my actuarial tables say. The number's not far off from the psalmist, actually, who confidently assures me that the days of my life are seventy years, or eighty if I am lucky. But I know it can be gone in an instant.

Yes, our material possessions can also disappear without warning. Hurricanes and tornadoes rip homes apart. Lehman Brothers collapses; the pension vanishes. But such catastrophic events are rare. And anyway, it's stuff, which can often be replaced. What can't be replaced are people: the young mother cut down by cancer; the father of three on the verge of retirement, felled by an undiagnosed heart condition; the teenager in the car spinning out of control.

It feels macabre to bring up death in this way. Yet for me, it's the foundation of a faithful stewardship of time. God is eternal; we are beautifully and painfully not. Knowing I will die someday doesn't paralyze me; it animates me. If I am one without hope, I'm going to try to deny death or cheat it. If I can stand on my Christian hope, however, I don't need to fear death . . . but nor should I squander this gift God has given me.

This life is a gift, as full as it is—I'm fortunate to have good friends, satisfying work, hobbies that bring me joy, and children and a spouse who count on me, as I do on them. It would be a sad existence not to be needed by anyone, to have a calendar full of blank pages.

Still, even too much of a good thing can be too much. The groups I speak to are filled with people who feel like they could go all day every day and still not get it all done. Most people I know have already separated the wheat from the chaff on their schedules. They feel the real impact of letting even important stuff slide. They are juggling multiple worthwhile things, captive to the culture's relentless drive to do more and do it better. Many of them become time tacticians and master multitaskers, scheduling every minute, answering the work emails in the grocery store line, taking the conference call on the sidelines of the kids' swim meet. (I admit I have done both of those things.)

In retreats and gatherings I lead about my book *Sabbath in the Suburbs*, we talk a lot about the word *busy*. What's at stake when we use that word? Sometimes, admittedly, it's a neutral descriptor: "There's a lot going on, that's all. It's a hectic season of life." But too often the word becomes a yardstick we use to measure our own self-worth and the worth of others. James Surowiecki wrote recently in the *New Yorker* that 94 percent of white-collar workers worked fifty hours or more a week, and almost half of them work more than sixty-five hours a week. That's more than five, twelve-hour days. This is a shift from previous generations, in which lower-wage workers were the ones pulling the longest hours. "Overwork has become a credential of prosperity," Surowiecki concludes.[5] Busy has come to mean successful. Indispensable. Important.

We use our busyness to justify turning down opportunities rather than letting our no be no: "Normally I would be able to help, but I just can't. Too busy." We hide behind a crammed schedule rather than deal with messy relationships in need of attention or reconciliation. Or we see busyness as a way of earning leisure. "Work hard, play hard," the saying goes. Our Protestant work ethic tips over into works righteousness: "Have I done enough to deserve some time off?" And yet God doesn't audit our to-do list to make sure we've accomplished enough before we can take a Sabbath, go on vacation, or retire. It's time to rest when it's time to rest.

Stewardship of time is tied closely into stewardship of the body. How much work is too much? At what point does the body break down? The Japanese have a word, *karoshi*, which literally means "death from overwork," and some observers estimate that hundreds of Japanese people die a year from the condition.[6]

I once confronted the connections between time stewardship and stewardship of the body, when I sustained an injury while training to run my second marathon. Some of it was simple bad luck—you can do everything right as a runner and still get hurt. But my injury stemmed partly from overtraining, especially taking on too much, too fast. Maybe in a younger body I would've been okay, but I bit off more miles than this middle-aged body could safely chew. I made the same mistake with my training plan that many of us do with our schedules: overestimating our energy level, underestimating the toll it will take, and fooling ourselves that if it all fits on the calendar then it's totally doable. Add a willingness to ignore the early warning signs of burnout, and it's a recipe for disaster.

My body put the brakes on my ambitious plans in a way that was inelegant but effective: a tibial stress fracture, a tiny crack in my leg bone that healed only when I was forced to rest by a stern doctor and the knowledge that pushing it would only make things worse. I resented the three-month hiatus from running, and gritted my teeth as marathon day came and went without me on the course. That's the dirty little secret of stewarding your time well: even when you take a break, life goes on without you. The world doesn't stop when you do. Rest time is rarely affirmed, and when it is, it can seem patronizing: "Aww, good for you, taking time off!" say the Type-A warriors as they speed by.

But what is the alternative? We have only this one life. We have to take care of it. In my case, I had no choice if I wanted to continue this practice that has brought me joy and community, to say nothing of physical health. My mantra during my three-month break was "I'd rather be running at 90 than run in the next 90 days."

Now that I'm back on the road and the trails, I've had to change the way I train. Gone are the weeks in which I'd run five days. Now it's three days at most, plus some cross-training here and there. Such is the intersection between stewardship of time and stewardship of the body—a constant toggling between delight in the present and an eye toward the future. Too much of the former can lead to hedonism; too much of the latter leads to workaholism.

For years, people have talked about how to find the elusive work/life balance. I'm heartened that the language is changing—more and more people I meet have let go of the language of *balance* and are seeking out other metaphors. Balance feels too precise to many of us, like a ballerina standing *en pointe* or a tightrope walker making her painstaking way across the rope. Balance is beautiful to watch, but it's not a realistic life goal; *wholeheartedness* is better. Life is too fluid, chaotic even, for balance. Instead, I am seeking to be present. When it's time to work, I work, and when it's time to play with my kids, I want to do my best not to be thinking about work. Perhaps Ecclesiastes 3 is as helpful a text as we're likely to find for stewardship of time. There is a time for every purpose under heaven. Our primary work, then, is always to discern what time it is.

All of us are called to this work of discernment, regardless of our religious background. But those of us who do this work in Christian community have particular challenges. First, we are good at talking out of both sides of our mouths on stewardship of time. We may preach Sabbath and self-care; we may require church officers to take a year off between terms; we know that burnout is a possibility for even the most energetic and passionate church volunteers. On the other hand, the third-grade Sunday school isn't going to teach itself. The nominating committee is stumped because everyone has said no, but Stalwart Steve has agreed to serve—again. And Sunday's coming as it stubbornly does, and the people are going to show up expecting a sermon and a prayer and a choir anthem.

Our second challenge is that pastors are some of the worst offenders when it comes to finding a life-giving rhythm to their days. I have attended many denominational gatherings honoring pastors on their retirement, and I cringe whenever the pastor thanks the long-suffering spouse for dealing with the missed birthdays and anniversaries while the pastor was serving the church. Granted, ministry does not conform to a time clock. People have emergency surgery or die or get arrested for drunk driving irrespective of the pastor's family calendar. But I have friends whose chief goal in ministry is not to have to apologize to their families at the end of it. Such goals are easier made than kept, of course. A friend who pastors a large church told me not long ago that, while he did manage a vacation with some regularity, it had been years since he'd had a full day off. *Years.* Yet we can lead others only as far as we ourselves have been led. As pastors, we don't need to have it all figured out, but we do need to strive for congruence between what we preach and what we live.

If we have particular challenges in discerning "what time it is," then we also have rich resources that guide us in this work. A stewardship of time is well served by appreciating sabbath, *chronos*, and *kairos*; respecting our calendars; and furthering our sense of scale.

Sabbath

From my experience speaking and preaching about Sabbath, it appears most Christians associate Sabbath with the story of creation. God made the universe and everything in it, and then rested for a time. God did it, so we do it. The rhythm is established. But for Jews, the story of liberation from slavery looms larger. The Sabbath day is a gift for the

Jewish people because it reminds them of the time when they were captive to Pharaoh's command, when their ancestors were forced to work, not six days a week, but every day of the week. There was no freedom, no relief, just the constant expectations of doing more, producing more, and building more. Thus the Jewish observance of Sabbath is more than a pause. It is an exclamation to the world: "We are not slaves to the empire anymore!"

It's problematic to suggest that affluent Americans are "slaves" to overwork. When someone complains about how stressed and busy they are, my friend Deryl Fleming likes to say with a wink, "Let me see your calendar . . . hmm, this all looks like your own handwriting." We often bring it on ourselves, and there is no comparison to true slavery. Still, my pastor's heart grieves with the parents who feel like their children get the dregs of their time and energy after the paid work is done, or the ones who see promotions and opportunities pass them by because they're unwilling or unable to work the punishing hours required. I hear the stories of caring for an aging parent to the exclusion of everything else. I feel the heaviness from people who'd like nothing more than to silence the cell phone once in a while. But in an office culture in which the boss expects a quick answer to every email, they feel stuck. It's not slavery, but it is a kind of spiritual captivity.

Sabbath steps into this breach, though not with easy answers. From experience, I have to admit that practicing Sabbath doesn't mean everything else clicks into place. There isn't suddenly enough time for the many competing concerns of our lives. What sometimes happens, however, is that Sabbath becomes a delivery mechanism for God's grace. It provides space and perspective, even if the laundry is still waiting for us at the end. While the riddle of how to spend our time is always with us, Sabbath offers a powerful reminder that we are not indispensable to the running of the world, and that God's steadfast love is available to us, empowering us, even when we've stepped off the hamster wheel of activity (maybe especially then).

Chronos and *Kairos*

"Don't blink—it goes by so fast." It's the rare parent of young children who hasn't been hit with that advice by more seasoned parents. It's not wrong. But it's not always helpful either. Yes, the years fly by, but the days are often long, and sometimes, they are best endured and forgotten rather than cherished. "Savor this time" becomes an additional burden of guilt on the hard days when nothing is going right.

I marvel at the passage of time and how it shows itself in the people around me—the crinkles deepening around my husband's eyes, the dimple on my thirteen-year-old's face that hasn't changed since she was three, or the top of my son's head that won't fit under my own chin much longer. But I can't marvel at these things all of the time; I've got stuff to do.

The Bible describes this reality using two Greek words for time, *chronos* and *kairos*. *Chronos* is clock time, measured in minutes, hours, and days. *Kairos* is holy time—God's time, God's appointed season.

It's a comfort to me that the writers of scripture acknowledge that not all *chronos* is *kairos*. Here is the story of God's people, engaged in the quotidian beauties of life—eating, working, traveling, loving, birthing, planting, dying—and while God is always with them, not all of it is *kairos*. *Kairos* is reserved for God's decisive action, the inbreaking of Christ that transforms our lives. *Kairos* can happen in the big moments and turning points. But sometimes the holiness sneaks up on us too. It's not only the wedding, but the unexpected conversation in the car on the way home from school.

I wonder how a fuller exploration of *chronos* and *kairos* might inform our stewardship of time. As a culture, too often we numb ourselves through food, work, shopping, or the Internet, while simultaneously craving excitement and stimulation like an addict jonesing for a hit. Can we learn together to be attentive for moments of *kairos* without expecting that holiness will show up whenever it suits us?

In this era of smartphones, we have the ability to capture any and every moment for posterity, but just because we can doesn't mean we should. I shake my head at piano recitals and school assemblies as parents sit holding their iPads in front of their faces, recording their children instead of watching them in real time. For what purpose do we make such exhaustive archives? As comedian Jim Gaffigan quips, "I have more pictures of my children than my father ever looked at me."[7] Yes, there is a social nature of sharing these moments with our loved ones, especially online. But why are we constantly recording and chronicling our lives? Have we become so thirsty for *kairos* that we think we'll find it in some random JPG or mp4 file? I'd rather have my eyes open to see it the first time.

Calendars as Theological Documents

Many a church leader has argued that our checkbooks are actually theological documents. What we give our money to communicates something about who we are and what we believe. Do we give generously from our financial resources? Do we tithe, or are we working toward a tithe? Do we give only if there's money left over, or is giving to the church a priority we make room for before other things? As uncomfortable as these questions can be, we're used to asking them in the church. Many a stewardship campaign has been built around Jesus' reminder, "Where your treasure is, there will your heart be also" (Matt. 6:21).

But our time can be as much a treasure as our finances. I'd like to see the church talk about our calendars as theological documents as well:

- *What do we give our time to?* Do we intentionally make time for spiritual practices, or do we simply hope they will happen? Are we setting aside time for exercise, time with family and friends, and rest? Even the way we frame the activity makes a difference. Do we understand Sunday school and church as time with God—an investment in our discipleship—or just another activity among many?

- *Are we minding our margins?* Do we pack our calendars full, or do we provide adequate space in our schedule for the holy interruptions that inevitably occur? Are we overscheduling our children, cramming their lives full of enrichment, or are we allowing them to engage in unstructured play? Time for boredom and daydreaming is key to a child's development; they don't get the chance to develop these skills when we over-program their time.
- *Are we attentive to the seasons?* The liturgical year is a priceless resource to a culture addicted to excitement and novelty. In a world dominated by 24/7 media and the scandal du jour, we dare to preach the importance of quiet waiting and patient expectation, of letting a moment ripen. As the society around us binges on Christmas, we sing Mary's defiant song of liberation for the poor. When the news dishes out one distressing story after another, we proclaim Christ's resurrection, not just on a single day but for the long vibrant season of Eastertide.

Conversations about personal finances are incredibly fraught in the church; it's the rare congregation that can have them and have them well. Perhaps churches might get some practice by talking about time instead. I'd like to see members of small groups do discernment around one another's schedules, holding one another accountable to a more gentle way of living.

A Sense of Scale

My daughter is taking part in a performance of *The Lion King* at her middle school, so the soundtrack is on high rotation in our house. I've loved the musical for years, and involuntarily tear up when Simba finally takes on his father's mantle and assumes the kingship of Pride Rock, a role he's been resisting for much of his life. For a story that began as a Disney movie for kids, it has surprisingly deep archetypes and resonances.

"He lives in you," the chorus sings to Simba, referring to his fallen father, gone but always with him.[8] Simba is connected to the great "Circle of Life."

At the same time, I'm always struck by the line in that song that says, "There is more to see than can ever be seen. / More to do than can ever be done."[9] I'm touched by the paradox that, while we are connected to the eternal in powerful ways, we ourselves are finite, painfully restrained in what we can experience in this life.

That sentiment is Psalm 90 theology: "LORD, you have been our dwelling-place / in all generations. / Before the mountains were brought forth, / or ever you had formed the earth and the world, / from everlasting to everlasting you are God" (vv. 1–2). And also: "The days of our life are seventy years, / or perhaps eighty, if we are strong; / even then their span is only toil and trouble; / they are soon gone, and we fly away" (v. 10).

The eternal God is our dwelling place. But God's eternity doesn't give us unlimited time. We need Psalm 90 when we're tempted to inflate our own importance. We need it when we think we're in control—ever. We need it when we fall into what one writer called the messiah trap: "If I don't do it, it won't get done, and everyone else's needs are more important than mine."

We also need it when we're tempted to stress over the small stuff. Writer Anne Lamott tells the story of shopping for a dress with her friend Pammy, who was dying of cancer. Anne turned around in the dressing room, and said, "Do you think it makes my hips look big?" Pammy looked back at her with great love, and said, "Annie? I really don't think you have that kind of time."[10]

When I lead groups in Bible study on the Sabbath, we look at the creation story and God's observance of a day of rest. We often pause over the line "And on the seventh day God **finished the work that he had done**, and he rested on the seventh day from all the work that he had done" (Gen. 2:2, emphasis added). "Must be nice!" they say with a laugh. Our work seems never done, and will never be done. There will always be books unread, words unspoken, plans unfulfilled, bucket lists unfinished. The key is to be as intentional as we can with the time we have, and to trust the everlasting grace of God, who never ends.

In his book *Leadership Jazz*, Max De Pree talks about the construction of New College, Oxford in the fourteenth century. The quadrangle provided all the services the students needed, with the chapel and the great hall as the crowning achievements. About five hundred years later, the buildings had begun to deteriorate—the giant oak beams that supported the structure had started to rot. Architect Sir Gilbert Scott was enlisted to help, and with a group from the college visited Great Hall Woods in Berkshire. There he found trees that had been planted a hundred years before, specifically planted to be replacement beams when the time came and the need arose. They'd been growing large and strong for a century, waiting for the opportunity to be used to make an ancient building sturdy and beautiful again.[11]

As a church, we don't build many cathedrals anymore, let alone 10,000-year clocks. But with God's help, we should be planting trees—both mindfully and recklessly, carefully and abundantly—to sustain and shelter generations we will never see.

Questions for Reflection

1. Examine your personal calendar as if it were a theological document. Where do you spend most of your time? What do you prioritize? Does your calendar align with your faith convictions and values?

2. Examine your congregation's calendar as a theological document. What shows up on the church calendar? What does this suggest about your priorities and commitments? Who is involved and invited? How might you consider what's taking place beyond the church walls?

3. What are your experiences, if any, with Sabbath? How might your life shift to embrace stewardship of time more fully?

Applications for Life Together

- Consider implementing or experimenting with the following practices that help cultivate deep presence and stillness: meditation, yoga, technology-free areas or times, *lectio divina*, contemplative music, labyrinth walking, or spending time in nature.
- Create a chronological timeline of your life (e.g., birth, graduation dates, moves, jobs). Create a second timeline that depicts *kairos* time, or life events (e.g., baptisms, births, particular work of the Spirit). Consider the places of overlap and lack thereof. What do you make of the differences and similarities?

2

Stewardship of Life at Its End

"Receive the Sign of the Cross"

MARY HINKLE SHORE

When my father and one of his physicians were considering the implications of a metastatic cancer diagnosis, Dad asked the doctor, "Am I terminal?" and the doctor replied, "We're all terminal." My parents received this response as singularly unhelpful. Was the doctor trying to make a joke? Was he trying to be philosophical? The quip did not find an appreciative audience, yet the doctor's words were accurate. So then, since we are all terminal, what does it mean to be stewards of our own lives or another's as it nears its end? As we approach our own death and as we accompany others, how can Christians care faithfully for what has been entrusted to us?

As I prepared to write, I mentioned the topic to a few people, and I was surprised at the ground they expected the essay would cover. "Are you going to discuss the percentage of health care dollars spent in the last few weeks of life?" someone asked. I heard, "Will you talk about physician-assisted suicide?" A third person expected that "stewardship at the end of life," meant suggesting ways to dispose of one's assets faithfully. It had not occurred to me to engage any of these topics. After they were suggested, I could see their connection to concerns about the call to stewardship. Certainly

16

medical professionals, financial advisors, attorneys, and public health advocates all have roles in helping us practice good stewardship as incapacity and death approach.

My focus, however, is on *the stewardship of people and relationships as it is practiced by a congregation at the end of a person's life.* Here I review core Christian convictions about death, resurrection, community, and God's presence with the suffering; and I explore how our embodiment of these convictions is an act of stewardship. As stewards, we proclaim that (1) in holy baptism, we are joined to the death and resurrection of Christ; (2) to be in Christ is to belong to a body with many members; and (3) God's self-revelation on the cross confirms that God suffers with us, redeems loss, and will raise us up (again) with Christ.

With my focus on these elements of the gospel, I am not implying that we arrive singly or in groups at a brother's or sister's bedside and launch into pronouncements on the topics of baptism, Christian community, and a theology of the cross. I have something more dynamic in mind. Nonetheless, a review of what we say we believe may be helpful. I begin with such a review and conclude by describing practices that embody these beliefs.

Dead Already

In *From the Parish for the Life of the World*, Stephen Bouman tells the story of his maternal grandfather, who was "passionate about three things above all: the Greek New Testament, fishing, and Baptism." At his funeral liturgy, "One of the speakers recalled some of Grandpa's word about Baptism. Among them was this sentence, heard first by me with a fishing pole in my hand: 'In your Baptism, the only death you need to fear is already behind you.'"[1]

The apostle Paul put it this way:

> Do you not know that all of us who have been baptized into Christ Jesus were baptized into his death?

> Therefore we have been buried with him by baptism
> into death, so that, just as Christ was raised from the
> dead by the glory of the Father, so we too might walk
> in newness of life.
>
> For if we have been united with him in a death like
> his, we will certainly be united with him in a resurrec-
> tion like his. (Rom. 6:3–5)

In holy baptism, Christians confess that we are mystically joined to the death of Christ. The life of the baptized, then, is the practice of exploring the freedom of having, on the one hand, nothing left to lose, and, on the other hand, an eternity of life to give away. In the 1993 movie, *Groundhog Day*, Phil (played by Bill Murray) discovers that no matter what happens on any day, the next morning he will wake up again to the same song on the radio, and the same day to live over and over again. He changes things up each day, trying to escape the cycle, even by doing things that get him killed several times. Every morning he wakes again. Eventually, he starts using his knowledge of the day for good. In each new iteration of the day, Phil shows up at the right time to catch a boy about to fall out of a tree; he learns to play the piano; and after much practice, he is the best version of himself in a relationship with Rita (Andie McDowell). Phil spends many, many days discovering how to live one day well.

Those who are baptized have a similar kind of freedom and future. Nothing worse than death alongside the Crucified One—already done—can happen to you. Throughout life, those who remember that they are "already dead" have less to defend, less to prove, less to attempt to control, and less to fear. Baptism into Christ offers the freedom to live experimenting, failing, repenting, and being forgiven. It is the freedom to begin again and again. There is no need to protect, defend, or hoard the life of those who have died; the life of the baptized is for living and sharing eternally.

The freedom of having already died is for living and also for dying. When the baptized approach death, we do so knowing our true life is in Christ rather than in all that one might assume needs to be defended: our honor or another's, our importance, our being beloved, our independence, our life.

Imagine just one way this awareness might change our living with illness and our dying. Perhaps Christians could speak about cancer with something other than battle language. The medical imagination around cancer treatment is still largely confined to "slash, burn, and poison," and obituaries regularly speak of someone's "courageous battle" with the disease—a battle always lost by the time the obituary is published. Might we instead speak of a brother's or sister's courageous endurance in the midst of suffering or his or her graceful living in the midst of dying? Those who know that the hold on creation of the "last enemy to be destroyed" is already unraveling do not minimize the reality of grief and sadness associated with the loss of one's own life or the life of someone we love. Yet we do bear witness that, as real as our losses are, we *live* (rather than merely battling) in the midst of them, and they are not ultimate.

Life Together

In the fourteenth chapter of Romans, Paul is impressing on his readers that freedom in Christ does not extend to judging others on the basis of certain faith practices. In words reminiscent of the idol-meat controversy in 1 Corinthians, Paul speaks about eating ("Some believe in eating anything, while the weak eat only vegetables," Rom. 14:2). He also speaks about observing special days ("Some judge one day to be better than another, while others judge all days to be alike," v. 5). After these specific examples, Paul states his more general point: "We do not live to ourselves, and we do not die to ourselves. If we live, we live to the Lord, and if we die, we die to the Lord; so then, whether we live or whether we die, we are the Lord's" (vv. 7–8).

To be "in the Lord" means to belong to Christ and to belong also to others in the body of Christ. Relationships within the body can become strained. Even so, the Christian life is a life lived in community. We do not live to ourselves.

This insight has implications for how we live as we near the end. A friend admits his impatience with people who are always saying they do not want to be a burden to their children. "As if our children were never a burden to us," he quips. Life consists of being and having burdens, and the Christian life consists of bearing one another's burdens (see Gal. 6:2).

Christians confess that long before we are numbered among those who need assistance with "activities of daily living,"[2] we know that independence is a lie. We are radically dependent on God and one another. At the end, it helps to have been long acquainted with the gifts that giving and receiving help can be.

Those baptized into Christ know that dependence upon others near our end is not shameful—no matter what other voices in our culture might say. It is not a sign of bad stewardship earlier in life. It does not represent a failure to plan appropriately or to die in a timely way. All of us have always needed others; the advantage Christians have is that we know it early and hear it often. Our need and God's provision are implied, even in the insight of stewardship education that "all is gift," and in the insight of the Protestant Reformation that we are saved by grace.

Good stewardship at the end of life is a practice of accepting help from others and offering it without dehumanizing or infantilizing a brother or sister. We give and receive help as members of one body rather than as some who are "independent" and others who are "ill."[3] This may mean accepting or offering help with activities of daily living, like eating or dressing. It may also mean receiving or offering help with the task of trusting God in the midst of experiences that frighten us. A friend explains in the family's Christmas letter that they received a cancer diagnosis: "The weeks that followed were a fog of grief, survived only because the community of faith kept reminding us of what we had said we believed over a lifetime." Together we live, even as we face death.

Life and Death with the God Who Suffers

In the Heidelberg Disputation of 1518, Martin Luther distinguished between the theologian of glory and the theologian of the cross.[4] The theologian of glory looks at the "tit-for-tat" quality of the world and projects reciprocity onto God: good is rewarded; evil is punished. But things did not work that way in the life of Jesus, and so a theologian of the cross does not expect that they will work that way in the lives of those who follow Jesus. Carl Trueman summarizes, "The fact that God humbled himself, took flesh, and died a painful death . . . is itself a powerful revelation of who God actually is and how he acts. Christ's hanging on the cross is constitutive of the very identity of God toward fallen human beings."[5] God, though hidden, is fully present in the event of Christ's crucifixion and redeems not only the righteous sufferer but the whole creation through this event. Therefore God, though hidden, may be expected to be fully present and working redemption wherever there is suffering.

Douglas John Hall makes the point more simply:

> In short, the cross is more about God's suffering *with* us than it is about God's suffering *for* us.
>
> . . . The gospel of the cross tells of the *Mitleid* ["suffering with"] of One who, fearfully and at great cost, assumes our human destiny fully, following it through the bitter end, and seeking to alter it day after day, not *from above* but *from within* the seething crucible of creaturely life and history. . . . Even on this lonely blue planet wandering in infinite space; even in the empty spaces of our personal wonderings . . . "we are not alone."[6]

We are not alone when we suffer, not even when we feel as forsaken in suffering as Jesus did on the cross (see Mark 15:34). Suffering is not a synonym for punishment, and undeserved suffering is not proof that our lives are meaningless. In suffering, God is with us—for good.

This news cautions those who believe suffering is meaningful only if people are responsible for their own ailments, or if blame may be otherwise assigned. (We may think we are enlightened beyond such responses, but how different are we from Job's friends when we discreetly seek or share information about whether someone diagnosed with lung cancer was a smoker?) The sufferer's friends will steward their gifts and their friend well, not by combing through the evidence for how reciprocity is at work, but by remaining compassionately present in another's suffering as God is present, and by confessing that the world makes sense on different terms than simply that good is rewarded and evil punished. Indeed, "Has not God made foolish the wisdom of the world? . . . For God's foolishness is wiser than human wisdom, and God's weakness is stronger than human strength" (1 Cor. 1:20, 25). Such are the conclusions of a theologian of the cross.

For those who accompany sufferers, faith in the God who suffers curbs the impulse of the well to distance themselves from the sick in order to convince themselves that, "It couldn't happen to me." And to those who are suffering, such faith offers hope in the midst of circumstances that could otherwise lead to despair.

As we near the end of our lives or another's, these convictions help to shape our care for one another:

1. Having been buried with Christ in baptism, we know death already, and we know what it is to share in the life of the Risen One.
2. We exist always with and for one another, in the communion of saints across time and place and in the community of Christ's body as it exists in a local congregation.
3. The God revealed in Christ is a God who suffers with us and all creation, as it and we groan, awaiting redemption (see Rom. 8:22–23).

Congregational stewardship of one who is near death embodies these convictions with the practices of prayer to a compassionate God, accompaniment in the midst of circumstances that threaten to isolate, and the commendation of the beloved one to the God who ever creates life out of death.[7]

Prayer

A friend in the southern United States speaks of prayer within her tradition, "I offer prayer the way I might offer you a cool drink if you stop by my home on a warm day." In other parts of the United States, and in more reticent Christian traditions, we are often afraid to pray with others. We worry about everything: Will they be offended if we suggest prayer? What if they are mad at God? What should we pray *for* when one is in the midst of something incurable? What if we start and get stuck, or fall silent, or cry?

The word for stewards here is "muddle through." People need cool drinks on warm days. Pray. Invoke the presence of God in all circumstances.

Prayer may be practiced by means of silence, song, speech, or a combination of these. Words can come from Scripture: many of the psalms are prayers, as are other scriptural words, like "I believe; help my unbelief" (Mark 9:24) and "let this cup pass from me" (Matt. 26:39) and "Lord, have mercy" (17:15; 20:30). Or words can come from hymns, or other elements of the tradition, or the heart. Together, we intercede, lament, wait for God, make confession and receive forgiveness, and offer praise and thanksgiving.

Lament

Because it is often overlooked, and because grief—and the feelings of anger, unfairness, and loss grief inspires—is so often part of our last days, the practice of lament deserves special attention here.[8] The simplest lament is, "Why?" and it is a prayer. Why? Why me? John Swinton observes,

> Lament, and in particular psalm-like lament, is the cry of the innocent, the one who feels treated unfairly,

who feels that God has somehow not lived up to the
sufferer's covenant-inspired expectations. . . . It is . . .
a . . . form of prayer that is not content with soothing
platitudes or images of a God who will listen only to
voices that appease and compliment. Lament takes
the brokenness of human experience into the heart of
God and demands that God answer.[9]

The psalms are perhaps our most useful resource here as
prayers and a template for prayer.

> How long, O Lord? Will you forget me forever?
>   How long will you hide your face from me?
> How long must I bear pain in my soul,
>   and have sorrow in my heart all day long?
> How long shall my enemy be exalted over me?
>   Ps. 13:1–2

The psalm goes on like that for a while, eventually ending
with an expression of praise for the Lord's goodness, though
perhaps even the confession of faith in God's goodness is a
reminder to God to step up!

In his chapter on lament as the practice of resistance and
deliverance, Swinton borrows from the work of Ann Weems
and Bill Gaventa to illustrate how Christians can create new
lament psalms that are prayers for ourselves and others in
suffering.[10] Those writing new psalms may be helped by the
structure Swinton offers, summarized here:

1. Lament psalms are addressed to God. One may choose
   to name God in many different ways.
2. Lament psalms contain a complaint (or several!).
3. Lament psalms express trust. The complaint is vivid
   precisely because the one who prays trusts that God
   has her best interests at heart.
4. Lament psalms make an appeal. They are a way of saying to God, "Act!"

5. Lament psalms usually include a statement of faith that God will indeed act on behalf of the psalmist.

6. Lament psalms usually include a promise of praise. The psalmist announces that she will offer praise for deliverance, or the community speaks a promise of God's faithfulness into the ears of the sufferer.

Confession and Forgiveness

Stewards seek to repair what is broken. Whether it happens at the end of a day, or in a few moments of silence in Sunday morning worship, or as we approach our death, a review of life reveals our distance from the new life to which the baptized are called. Hospice literature counsels that we all have a few simple things to say and hear as we near death. Among them are the words, "I'm sorry" and "I forgive you." Rites of confession and forgiveness put these words on our lips and in our ears as prayer.

Praise and Thanksgiving

Now thank we all our God with hearts and hands and voices,
who wondrous things has done, in whom this world rejoices;
who, from our mothers' arms, has blest us on our way
with countless gifts of love, and still is ours today.[11]

The end of life also offers opportunities for prayers of praise and thanksgiving. Whenever we take time to look back, we see the gifts that others have been to us and the blessings God has offered throughout our lives. Alongside "Help," and the other elements of lament, our prayers at this time often include "Thanks" and "Wow."[12] The best resources for praise and thanksgiving are often familiar hymns. Using hymn texts as prayers frees those who fear having to make words up as they go along. One or two people can sing, and so can the church choir bunched into a corner of a care facility's dining hall and accompanied by a piano as hobbled as the residents. The practice of prayer in the form of song connects us to long-held memories often still intact when other capabilities have failed us. Singing our prayer, we steward all that has been and whatever is left.

Accompaniment

In 1 Corinthians 10, Paul is reviewing the ups and downs of Israel's time in the wilderness as an analogue for what the predominately Gentile church in Corinth is going through, and he writes, "So if you think you are standing, watch out that you do not fall. No testing has overtaken you that is not common to everyone. God is faithful, and he will not let you be tested beyond your strength, but with the testing he will also provide the way out so that you may be able to endure it" (1 Cor. 10:12–13). All occurrences of "you" in this section of the letter are plural. Paul clearly addresses himself to the community here and not to individuals. In recent years, however, the text is almost always referred to by people as if it were addressed to individuals experiencing suffering or temptation.

In a talk at the Wild Goose Festival in 2013, Nadia Bolz-Weber rejected this standard interpretation. Blogger Eric Smith remembers,

> At the end of her talk, Nadia talked about church as the cure for Western individualism run amok. "It's not about you," she chided. That old expression, vapid as it is common, that "God doesn't give you anything you can't bear?" That's crap, and it ignores the value of an embodied community, the value of a Body of Christ. "God doesn't give you anything a community can't bear," she said. No one can bear everything alone. But when you're part of a body, anything is possible.[13]

We steward people and relationships within Christian community as we show up for one another throughout our lives and at their ends. We accompany one another. Sometimes accompaniment means going to soccer games when we have no idea how the game is played. Sometimes accompaniment means helping to carry the belongings of a refugee family up three flights of stairs. As someone's life nears its end, accompaniment means showing up when others are too frightened or repulsed by someone's circumstances to appear. When my father neared the end of his life, a neighbor appeared once a week to sit with him so my mom could spend a few hours in the yard and garden. Seeing the hospital bed and portable toilet in the family room, and watching week after week as my dad's skeleton seemed to dissolve from bone cancer was too frightening for some of his friends. Many of them stayed away, but a few of them appeared, and those who did made my dad's last weeks bearable for both my parents.

The power of death is chiefly its power to break relationship or enforce separation. Likewise, the power of suffering, pain, and illness is the power to isolate. By showing up for one another, we bear witness to our common life and testify to the limits of any isolating experience to separate us from one another and from God.

How can we be present for each other? Sometimes it is as simple as dropping off dinner. In Richard Lischer's memoir, *Stations of the Heart,* the Duke Divinity School homiletics professor recounts the illness and death of his son, Adam, when Adam was a young man and about to be a father. Lischer writes,

> From mid-April to the autumn of 2005 we cooked almost nothing. When we thanked God for food, we were actually giving thanks for the friends, students, and generous strangers who delivered prepared meals to our house (and Jenny and Adam's) virtually every day of the week. . . . Often our friends brought meals we had shared in their home during better days, and sometimes they stayed and joined us for dinner. . . .

That summer we arrived at the most basic level of dependency, that of receiving nourishment from the hands of others.[14]

We also accompany one another by holding space for conversation and stories. On the road to Emmaus, a stranger draws near to Cleopas and his companion and asks, "What are you discussing with each other while you walk along?" As they answer the stranger's question, the conversation turns to scripture, grief, suffering, and hopes destroyed. Still they talk. Later they recognize that these conversations are exactly the sort of thing with which the risen Jesus spends time (Luke 24:13–35).

By showing up and listening, we steward the library of life stories that are within the other, and we invite the Risen One to interpret them alongside us. "Tell me about your first job." "What do you remember about your grandfather?" Questions as simple as these offer a chance to make sense of the present and imagine the future in light of the past.

A number of resources exist to help us, from both secular sources and religious publishers. StoryCorps has posted a list of "great questions,"[15] and another list is published in "Life Review in Pastoral Counseling: Background and Efficacy for Use with the Terminally Ill."[16] The books *Remembering Your Story* and *The Story of Your Life* provide exercises for groups to compose spiritual autobiography together.[17]

Commendation

Paradoxically, Christian stewardship involves both caring for people and things, and letting them go. There comes a time when those near the end of life do not need another ride to the doctor or another home-cooked meal. The community acknowledges its own limits and commends its own dear one to the never-failing love of God.

The Order for the Commendation of the Dying is similar across Protestant traditions and has its origin in the *Book of Common Prayer*. An expanded order, created by the members of Lake Chelan Lutheran Church in Chelan, Washington, is forthcoming under the title *Peace at the Last*. It is a picture book that includes the rite against a backdrop of watercolor illustrations along with psalms and music appropriate to the occasion.[18]

Peace at the Last also makes explicit the central role of our first death in baptism for understanding our last death. Words and actions from "Welcome to Baptism," as it is known in *Evangelical Lutheran Worship*, are adapted for use with the dying.[19] The sign of the cross had been made several times over the body of the one being welcomed to baptism. Now, in the community's commendation of the dying one, the sign of the cross is made many times again, each time with a charge appropriate to the occasion:

> Receive the cross on your forehead, a sign of God's endless love and mercy for you.
>
> Receive the cross on your ears, that you may hear God's voice calling you to your eternal home.
>
> Receive the cross on your eyes, that you may see the glory of God face to face.
>
> Receive the cross on your lips, that you may sing praise to Christ with choirs of angels and the whole host of heaven.
>
> Receive the cross on your heart, that God may dwell there now and always.
>
> Receive the cross on your shoulders, that you may lay down the yoke you have borne, and put your burdens to rest.
>
> Receive the cross on your hands, that you may release this world and cling to Christ.
>
> Receive the cross on your feet, that you may dance in the company of the saints forever.[20]

We end where we began, with the only death we need to fear behind us in baptism.

> The resurrection of Jesus achieves its most document-able meaning in each new community's embrace of it.

When old adversaries are restored in love and kneel together at the Lord's Table, their reconciliation testifies not to the minister's counseling skills but to the God who raises the dead and calls into existence the things that are not. When a persecuted congregation defies the powers arrayed against it and remains faithful, Jesus is glorified once again and lifted up for all to see. We can't make him real, any more than we can make the wind blow or create life from nothing. But we have seen the Lord. We can participate in his risen life and testify to him in the community.[21]

The practice of faithful stewardship of life as life nears its end is a testimony to the resurrection of Jesus. When we accompany another toward death, we bear witness to the news that Jesus Christ has defeated the power of death. His risen life is ours throughout all our days, including our last. In Word, Sacrament, and acts of love, we remember this with and for one another, and so care faithfully for all that has been entrusted to us.

Questions for Reflection

1. How do people in your congregation speak of illness and death? Is it common to hear battle language as described in this chapter? Or does your speech imply graceful living in the midst of dying? How might we reframe our language to reflect freedom and life in the midst of suffering?

2. In what ways do you explore themes of lament as a community?

3. How do you think about "accompaniment" as a worshiping community? How do members of your congregation accompany one another? Where do you see themes of independence and interdependence in your life together?

Applications for Life Together

- Consider holding a series of adult education events on the stewardship of the end of life. Topics might include funerals, baptismal theology, wills and estate planning, hospice and palliative care, and language concerning death and dying.
- Write a letter to or have a conversation with a loved one about death and dying. How do the faith convictions claimed in the chapter help, or hinder, the conversation?

3

Stewardship of Money and Finances

Practicing Generosity as a Way of Life

DAVID P. KING

Stewardship concerns more than money, but too often in broadening the conversation, money is the main topic we are seeking to avoid. Could it be easier to discuss a stewardship of time, technology, or talents? At one level, those of us formed within faith communities feel that the stewardship of money is routine. With pledge cards, capital campaigns, tithes, and offerings, we feel there's not much new to add. Same song, different verse, as leaders seek to raise the budget and invite members to do their fair share. Yet at another level, it is not the pervasive money talk in the church that is the problem; rather, it is the fear of discussing finances at all. Money remains *the* taboo topic for American Christians. Anthropologists define a cultural taboo as "something so sacred, so powerful, that to touch it or even talk about it is to expose oneself to considerable danger."[1] For many of us, money squarely fits the definition. At the least, it is impolite public conversation. At most, it is a topic we seek to avoid at all costs. We would rather talk about sex and politics—anything else—other than money.

While many assume that money talk is pervasive in faith communities, rarely are these direct conversations that explore the influence of money in our lives. As we manufacture natural buffers to avoid discussing money directly, we also know that our relationship with money is perhaps one of the best windows into the practices of the Christian life. In my interviews with hundreds of Christian pastors and lay leaders, few disagree with the significance of the role our relationships with money plays in the faithful practice of individuals and institutions. Those same religious leaders, however, admit struggling mightily to integrate the stewardship of finances into a broader vision of faith formation. Yet those same laity also confess to craving guidance on how their working, spending, saving, and giving fit into their lives of faith. As long as the stewardship of finances is correlated in our minds as a necessary evil to raise the church budget, there is little incentive to broaden the conversation. As long as our personal finances remain simply the process of paying our monthly bills, or a topic so personal it is better left alone, then a holistic vision of stewarding our finances will receive little interest from people of faith.

Too often we allow these tensions to paralyze us and avoid anything other than surface-level money conversations. Few of us are comfortable talking about money, even if we deeply feel the financial anxieties that occupy the hearts and minds of those entrusted to our care. The disconnect only grows as we divide what we feel is sacred from the secular. Nothing is more secular or profane than money, right? Should we not keep spiritual (i.e., non-financial) work safe from "filthy lucre"? Did Jesus not turn the tables of the temple moneychangers, shouting, "'Take these things out of here! Stop making my Father's house a marketplace!'" (John 2:16)? In "cleansing" the temple, is Jesus not suggesting that commercial practices blemish sacred spaces? Do not those entering religious vocations take explicit vows of poverty in order to avoid secular lives and give full attention to the spiritual life of prayer and service?

While Jesus displays understandable anger when individuals desecrate sacred space for personal financial gain, and while taking monastic vows to separate oneself from certain aspects of worldly life is surely right for some, this is only one response in relating to money. If this is our only alternative, then money is profane and the marketplace is secular—something to guard against—at best a necessary evil. Of course, Jesus models a broader approach. He has more to say on money than anything else in scripture aside from the kingdom of God, yet Jesus never took up an offering (not counting loaves and fishes). The sacred/secular divide is a false dichotomy. Our stewardship of finances *is* a spiritual issue. Jesus knew the power that money can have in and over our lives.

The Christian tradition has always understood the powerful role that money plays in the lives of individual disciples and faith communities. We are right to take note that Paul does not claim "money itself" but "the love of money" as the root of all kinds of evil (1 Tim. 6:10). Yet I fear that, too often, in engaging themes of faith and money, we tend to focus on the extremes at either end of the spectrum. We look at prosperity gospel preachers, Creflo Dollar's Gulfstream jets or Joel Osteen's magnificent mansions, and most of us are clear that this is not the intersection of faith and finances that we would follow. At the other end of the spectrum are new monastic communities like Shane Claiborne and the Simply Way, taking voluntary vows of poverty and keeping a common purse. We might value these communities' commitments within the broader economic structures, but not recognize this as our own particular calling. For the majority of us somewhere else along this spectrum, how do we make sense of wealth and possessions as we strive to apply our faith in the marketplace day after day?

The Christian tradition has most often identified wealth as an instrument. Possessions are not evil in themselves, but the focus is rather how they are put to use. As Clement of Alexandria, a second-century church father, claims in a sermon on money:

> Riches are not meant to be thrown away. For they are possessions . . . and are put under our power, as material and instruments which are for good use to those who know the instrument. If you use it skillfully, it is skillful; if you are deficient in skill, it is affected by your want of skill.[2]

Money has utility. This is the essential question of steward-ship: how do we properly use these resources entrusted to us? While money is not evil in itself, it is also rarely neutral. Clement does see wealth as an instrument that can be used for good or evil, but he also fears that possessions themselves most often have a tendency to possess us.[3] This is Jesus' same caution to the wealthy that warns of the difficulty the rich may have in entering the kingdom of heaven (Matt. 19:24).

While our society makes clear that money *is* power, the Christian tradition reframes this notion to assert that money *has* power and can often have power over us. When we lift money out of its properly ordered space, then it begins to define us, determine our values, and measure our self-worth as well as our relationship with others. As stewards, yes, we are managing finances and not allowing finances to manage us, but our work is much broader. A holistic stewarding of our finances reshapes our attitudes toward wealth and pos-sessions, but it also shifts our relationships with one another while recasting our vision of the good life in the midst of the multiple economies in which we take part.

The mission of the Lake Institute on Faith and Giving at the Indiana University Lilly Family School of Philanthropy, where I serve, focuses on fostering greater understand-ing of the ways in which faith inspires and informs giving. Most often we do that by engaging with congregations and faith-based institutions on issues of stewardship, generosity, and fundraising. People often come expecting how-to tools to raise budgets and a silver bullet to fix declining revenues. They are at first taken aback when we tell them that fundrais-ing and stewardship are not about money. Instead, we focus on relationships, vision, and faith formation. Whether indi-viduals or institutions, I think the same is true of a general stewardship of finances. While there are clearly cases when resources are lacking for individuals and communities, the first place for most of us is not the management of money but rather our relationship with it. How do we think theologically about money? What are the stories that frame our history with money? In a consumer culture, how much is enough?

And confronted with countless opportunities, what are my particular passions, where I can invest my finances and my vocation in God's work in the world? Reframing stewardship holistically moves us beyond the maintenance of church buildings or balancing individual budgets. It leads us to consider reimagining our relationship with money as a central aspect of discipleship. It allows us to be truth-tellers, acknowledging the countless ways that our anxieties over money and the power it often has over us inhibit our ability to fully embrace the Christian life and community that we want to pursue.

Stewarding Our Finances—Learning by Giving

"We make a living by what we get, but we make a life by what we give." Attributed to Winston Churchill but probably penned years earlier, such wisdom relates to Christian stewardship. Far more than managing resources, stewardship is the way that disciples make a life, and giving away yourself and the resources God has entrusted to you is central to our formation within a life of faith. Doris Buffett, elder sister of Berkshire Hathaway CEO and philanthropist Warren Buffett, has given away millions of dollars to students in colleges and universities across the country, but she has not primarily funded student scholarships. Instead, her Learning by Giving Foundation gives $10,000 to courses taught across college curricula. Students learn about the needs in local communities, the work of agencies meeting those needs, and by the end of the semester the students agree where to give away their $10,000. Perhaps it's easier to give away someone else's money, but the foundation's goal is clear—we learn by giving.[4] This is true for us as individual Christians as well. We gain power over money and possessions in our lives as we hold them loosely by deliberately looking beyond ourselves and investing in others. We too learn by giving; our faith grows as we give ourselves away.

Researchers in the Lilly Family School of Philanthropy have been tracking Americans' giving for over fifty years. Our records show that Americans annually give away an average of 2 percent of their after-tax income. That percentage has remained remarkably constant for decades. If we could move this national 2 percent needle only slightly, it would have enormous impact on the work nonprofits could do in the world. The largest recipient of North American giving continues to be faith-based organizations. The giving to congregations, denominations, and missionary societies alone makes up 33 percent of all North American giving—by far the biggest piece of the philanthropic pie.[5] When we ask individuals to identify the organizations to which they give, we find that 73 percent of all American giving goes to a congregation or otherwise religiously identified organization.[6] It's clear that faith is a significant factor for many in their giving.

It is not only the fact that faith-based organizations attract the largest percentage of Americans' generosity; researchers also agree that religiosity is often the best predictor of giving. Those Americans engaged in religious practices and faith communities are more likely to give, they give more often, they volunteer more, and they give more to both religious and secular causes.[7] What researchers often do not understand, however, is why. I think it is actually the social relationships that are formed in community, the religious rituals and practices, as well as the moral commitments of our religious traditions that are central to the fact that religious Americans are wired to give. Faith can be a tremendous motivator for the giving and stewarding of resources, breaking down artificial divisions between sacred and secular spheres.

Yet, while our traditions have a number of built-in resources that help us see how stewarding our finances and giving ourselves away are an essential part of our life of discipleship, we still are shaped by many other cultures of which we are a part. Often, an American individualist culture works against our religious traditions by emphasizing the necessity of achieving financial prosperity as the marker of success. And while we are seeking financial prosperity, the same consumerist culture portrays a sense of scarcity—that there is never enough and always something else we need. As consumers, we have no problem talking about money, and we proudly display labels and brands even as we brag about the deals we scored on Black Friday or Cyber Monday. Yet, maybe precisely because of the prevalence of money talk in our daily lives, these individualistic and consumer cultures often trump the call to stewardship from within our faith traditions and serve as barriers to generosity.

In studying congregations, sociologists of religion Patricia Snell Herzog and Brandon Vaidyanathan discovered three key obstacles to generosity.[8] *The first is wealth insecurity.* With the average American carrying over $5,700 in credit-card debt and mounting student-loan debts often reaching tens of thousands of dollars, financial anxieties are reality for many. These anxieties are dramatically evident for religious leaders, who find salaries and benefits provided for their work insufficient to provide for their families much less repay the significant debt many incurred through their professional theological education. When facing their own guilt, shame, and anger over their own financial situation, many pastors feel uncomfortable or inadequate discussing financial steward-ship. The result is that often we ignore or avoid these issues altogether. For others, our finances are sufficient to meet our needs, but we often live too close to the margins, wanting or desiring more than we need. For still others, our financial anxiety is a lack of general trust. Circumstances might always change, so we avoid giving, not out of a lack of desire, but out of a fear of unforeseen circumstances or future need. We cling tightly to our possessions in order to preserve our current or future way of life.

The second obstacle is giving illiteracy. Because of the taboo of money talk, our faith communities speak little about stewardship of finances and offer unclear expectations for those seeking guidance. Some traditions talk of a tithe, others ask engaged members to do whatever they can, still others ask for sacrificial gifts. Worried that we might offend, we speak in abstractions, and, therefore, many of us have little clarity as to what any standard of generosity might be.

Financial anxiety and fuzziness over expectations are concerns—whether real or imagined—but most worrisome is *the third obstacle that Herzog and Vaidyanathan label "comfortable guilt."* Most of us know that our faith requires us to give, but we are content to give just enough to make peace with our consciences that we are not giving more. We are too comfortable with the knowledge that our giving does not match our own expectations for what our faith tradition or personal values feel that we should give. Living amid the tensions that pull us in multiple directions, we too readily resign ourselves to the fact that we are not who we hope to be. Yet, if we submit to the notion that we make a life by what we give, and that the stewarding of our finances is central to our faith formation, then we cannot resign ourselves to doing just our fair share. Stewardship is not simply paying our dues; rather it is tending our souls so that we can see our wealth properly as an instrument to invest in God's kingdom. It is also working diligently to combat the subversive power money can often play in our lives, which causes us to believe that our net worth can be equated to our self-worth.

Organic Stewardship

When it comes to finances, Christian stewardship has often fallen into the trap of baptizing business-management language over deep engagement with the theology and practices of our own tradition. Despite the rich biblical language of stewardship, what we now take for granted as traditional annual pledging or capital campaigns only emerged alongside early twentieth-century American business practices. At the same time, nonprofit fundraisers began adopting stewardship language, as they talked about stewarding donors and institutional trust. Yet, if our only images of stewards are business managers and accountants, we may have fallen into the trap of believing that we simply co-opted *stewardship* from the business world. That presumption, however, undersells the centrality of a stewardship of finances within Christian discipleship.

Perhaps a more organic metaphor is fitting. What if stewards were more caretakers than managers? In Matthew 21,

Jesus offers us the parable of the tenants. The owner calls the steward (also translated "foreman") to organize and pay the workers. But beyond simply managing the affairs of his master, the steward is also called to watch over what has been entrusted to his care—both the individuals and the land. Stewards are more than task masters and paper pushers; they are nurturers. Like good parents and mentors that seek to nurture the unique gifts of their children and students, this is our calling as stewards. A wise steward walks the vineyard, tending to the needs of individual grapevines or individual employees, knowing their needs are not the same. It's more art than science. And we, the church, are the *terroir*—the soil—in which the grapes take root and derive their distinct flavors. Cultures of financial stewardship must be tended in order to take root and grow. The environment and the end product might not always be the same, but they share the need for nurturing.

On the other side of the production process, we might also gravitate to an image of a steward as a *sommelier*. Trained as food and wine experts, sommeliers make sure their guests have a wonderful dining experience, pairing wine that complements food selections and distinct palates. They too are stewards. The power of money in our lives is too great to view stewardship as managing finances by simply moving money from one column to another. Stewardship is rather tending our souls, aware of our unique fears and desires; nurturing our relationships with money as it marks a way of life; and leading us to experience faithful living and the joy of giving.

Generosity as a Way of Life

If our images of financial stewardship extend beyond business management, they must also extend beyond money. As a taboo topic, it is easy to avoid money talk, but at the same time, it is also easy to limit stewardship merely to the nuts and bolts of financial exchange. So it is equally important to step outside of economic categories. Notre Dame sociologist Christian Smith purposefully defines generosity through a broader lens. In addition to financial giving and volunteering, he also measures relational generosity and neighborliness. In building community, inviting others into your home, loaning a tool, or sharing a meal, you exhibit generosity. It turns out that neighborliness goes hand in hand with the giving of time, talent, and treasure. In his recent book, *The Paradox of Generosity*, Smith names the paradox quite explicitly: despite economists' analysis of opportunity costs and laws of diminishing returns, the fact remains that the more we give, the more we receive; the more we hold tightly to what we have, the more we have to lose.[9] Smith identifies high levels of generosity leading to greater happiness, health, purpose, and better relationships. What Smith also identifies is the fact that generous Americans self-identify as generous, while those with lower levels of generosity are aware they do not measure up. Smith's point is that you cannot pretend to be generous simply to receive health benefits, gain more friends, or feel better. Likewise, the decision to live generously is not just a series of daily choices; it is more a way of life. At times, it is about the bottom line and measured outcomes. At other times, it is about our motivations—why we give. But most often, it is about the practices of our faith—how we live as we care for our souls and the souls of others around us. Day after day. Week after week. Realizing that this often leads us to living counterculturally, the practices of our faith lead us on the path to be organic stewards nurturing generosity over simply managing money.

Without stepping back from our claim that we make a life by *what* we give, a stewardship of finances also cannot avoid *how* we make a living. Yes, these are questions of vocation, but they also frame how we partner with God's work in the world. One of Americans' most popular quotations from scripture is not even in the Bible: God helps those who help themselves. While the majority of Americans attribute the quotation to Jesus in the Gospels rather than the rightful heir, Ben Franklin in his *Poor Richard's Almanac*, the misidentification may say more about a quintessentially American theology of vocation than about contemporary biblical illiteracy. Work hard, pinch pennies, pull yourself up by your bootstraps, and God will bless your efforts. Sounds good, but many of us have lived long enough to realize this is not always the case. The starting line is not the same for everyone. Some of us face barriers to success or opportunity that have nothing to do with our talents and work ethic, and they are often in direct contrast to our hopes and dreams. Stewarding finances is always more than individual reflection. It is also a justice issue that forces us to consider our place in relationship to our community, society, and economy.

When we do focus on our own individual vocation, however, stewarding finances must always be more than simply questions of how to dispense the resources that we have earned. In examining scripture, biblical scholar Mark Allan Powell notes that a stewardship of finances is as much an issue of how we acquire, regard, manage, and spend our money as it is of how we give.[10] Opportunities for a bigger paycheck or a particular career choice might lead us into practices or away from commitments we have made as to how we hope to live. Quite often, our regard for money is the biggest stumbling block. Sometimes we harbor resentment because we feel entitled to more—if professional athletes and hedge-fund managers make millions, why do we not equally value teachers, pastors, and social workers? Of course, the resentment is often closer to home. Why am I making less than the person in the office next door when I work harder or feel that I am more valuable to the organization? Other times, our regard for money is founded in fear, anxiety, or envy, as we lose sleep worrying about having enough or not having as much as others. That often leads us to manage and spend our money in ways counter to a way of generous living. Beyond responsible saving, we hoard resources for fear of running out. Or we squander resources on things of little lasting value because we feel we deserve them, they make us feel good, or we simply seek to keep up with those around us. Our giving, then, is not how we invest what remains from what we have accumulated and left unspent; rather it is an extension of generosity built upon a foundation of our full relationship with money as a way of life. In other words, stewardship is how we share money, but also how we acquire, spend, invest our resources—our full experience with the gifts God entrusts to us.

New Measurements:
From Transaction to Transformation

We have a tyranny of measurement when it comes to financial stewardship. Within churches, we measure attendance, programs, annual budgets, and giving trends. When we focus on these measures alone, our narratives are often misguided. If general trend lines point down, we lament a narrative of decline as budgets shrink, attendance declines, and churches close. We look at envy or resentment at the communities with numbers trending up as they add staff or start new campuses; and we ask what they have done so that we can replicate their success. At other times, we acknowledge that their road to success is not possible or appropriate for our contexts. These scorecards are necessary in some form, but our infatuation with numbers must not be primary; far too often it leads us to false narratives of either decline or growth. We sink into despair and ascribe to the self-fulfilling prophecies that our time has passed, or we find comfort in the status quo, assuming steady growth as long as trends continue.

Of course, measured in this way, financial stewardship remains a means to an end. The fix to declining budgets as well as growing institutions is more money, and the way we ask people to give is most often through a sense of obligation. The church takes the National Public Radio approach. If you are a listener, particularly if you are still listening during the pledge-drive, you should do your part, make a pledge, and do your fair share. If you do nothing, you should feel guilty that others are footing the bill. Our local station incentivizes us with coffee cups, bumper stickers, or, better yet, the promise to stop asking and returning to regularly scheduled programming early if we would just help them meet their goal. Too often the church follows the same pattern, asking its members simply to pay their fair share toward the budget. Giving to the community sounds like an obligation and a biblical command of all Christians. This approach, whether by NPR or the church, may succeed in securing a donation, but it misses the larger opportunity to nurture generosity. For stewardship made whole, giving is a way of life. Framing giving as discipleship shifts the paradigm from the needs of our institutions to the passions and practices of individuals. We have refocused from transactional to transformational giving.

Relational Giving

If we consider how giving transforms our living, we soon realize that it is most often through relationships. Giving is not a solitary affair. For every gift giver, there is a recipient. Yet, most often, that giving relationship too is a transactional one. Think about gift giving at Christmas. Of course, you might give presents to your kids, spouse, or grandkids, which you know will be treasured because of your special insight into what they love or the simple fact that the gifts came from a loved one. Yet for every treasure that conjures up the chill bumps of O. Henry's *Gift of the Magi*, there are two office gift swaps and a white elephant exchange. Much of our giving is simply obligatory or reciprocal. Your next-door neighbor gives you something, or your office co-workers buy you a Starbucks gift card, and you feel the need to reciprocate. Sometimes you even find yourself, last minute, running to Walgreens to find something, anything you can give at the office party in return. While there is nothing wrong with trading holiday gifts at the office per se, most often it falls short of nurturing generosity. Reciprocating a gift is good manners and often culturally appropriate, but it does not make a way of life. Contrast it to a gift for a lover—you might save for months or years to purchase a diamond, a house, or a once-in-a-lifetime trip. Or for a child—every day you make lunches, wash clothes, and make other countless sacrifices. Just like neighbors' fruitcakes and colleagues' Starbucks gift cards, these gifts are also predicated on a relationship, but the difference is that you are glad to give without expecting anything in return. A simple yes, a smile on their faces, or an occasional "I love you" makes it all worthwhile.

Generosity is formed through relationships, but those relationships expand beyond simply giving from one person to another. They are also formed through community. Good giving requires a web of support and traditions, as well as communal responsibility and accountability. Through the lens of community, giving is also tied to issues of justice. Medieval Jewish rabbi and philosopher Maimonides (1135–1204 CE) makes this clear in his ladder of giving, adopted from his *Laws Concerning Gifts to the Poor* and still in use almost a millennium later. First, Maimonides reminds us that the Jewish *tzedakah*, often translated "charity" but probably better translated "justice" or "righteousness," is an essential aspect of Jewish life. Second, he acknowledges that while all *tzedakah* is good, some giving is better; he delineates eight levels of giving. Third, he notes these levels are built upon relationships—moving from anonymous giving to long-term relationship and from a short-term handout to walking alongside a neighbor "strengthening him until he needs to ask help of no one."[11]

If Maimonides' levels of giving are based on relationships, they also lead us to consider if our giving helps or hurts the individuals and communities that receive it. Recent bestsellers such as *Toxic Charity* and *When Helping Hurts* have awakened many Christians to what many social-service providers have reminded us for decades: our giving does not automatically help; it could also do damage.[12] Without dismissing the fact that most give with good intentions, some critics of traditional charity demonstrate that a large percentage of our charitable dollars are misguided or wasted when provided in the wrong form, at the wrong time, or to the wrong agencies. At other times, our giving might help meet immediate needs but inhibit the agency of recipients, leading to the perpetuation of need and bigger barriers erected between giver and recipient.

To be a good giver, we also need to know how to receive a gift. Do we know how to say thank you, to pause and

acknowledge that we have been the recipient of an undeserved gift without automatically working to return the favor
to avoid being in debt to another? Receiving a gift can make
us vulnerable and uncomfortable; it can also make us thankful. Is that not the story of the Christian faith, receiving a gift
in the form of Jesus Christ that we do not deserve? The life
of faith is rooted in and shaped by a wholeheartedly grateful
response to God's abundant generosity. Responding to God's
love leads us to participate in God's generosity toward others. That generosity is best practiced in community. How we
understand and live in relation to money, possessions, and
other kinds of goods depend on how we understand, live into,
and participate in the abundant life that God provides. Stewarding our finances is a key aspect of Christian discipleship,
and, therefore, we do not dare take away anyone's opportunity
to give. Giving is not the luxury of the wealthy; rather it is the
privilege of every person, which allows them to participate in
community and to live in response to God's generosity.[13]

Giving Reshapes Our Moral Imaginations

Giving reshapes our relationships with one another, with our
communities, and with God. Stewardship viewed in this way
also opens up our imaginations as to how we see the world.
Again, if it is true that we make a living by what we get, but we
make a life by what we give, then, when set free from the power
of money, we are able to see the world in new ways. Stewardship is less about legislating and fulfilling various moral rules;
instead, it is more about opening up our moral imaginations.
More than a positive mind-set, it is a new way of living out of
confidence and hope that notices abundance when others see
scarcity. Of course, this is never a Pollyannaish hope, but a hope
that gets our hands dirty working for change in the world.

  With such an outlook, we can look back and see the stories
of generosity that have shaped us throughout our lives. What
if, instead of a reminder to fill out your pledge card, the stewardship sermon asked us to reflect on one of these questions:

1. What is your earliest family memory of giving and volunteering?
2. Who have been some of your heroes and role models that reflect a generous life?
3. To what people and places do you feel a sense of gratitude?
4. What are the one or two life experiences that have shaped who you are today?
5. What is precious to you?
6. What values do you want to pass on to your family and friends?

It is important to look back and ask where we have been the recipient of gifts, how they affected us, and where our own passions and gifts lie.

In reflecting on generosity, we look back even as we also look ahead in reshaping our moral imaginations. Where we once saw need, we also see abundance. Stewards are first-class "noticers." They are generosity connoisseurs. They take delight in the generous acts of others. They seek out beauty, acknowledge it, and savor it wherever it appears. They attend to the assets in a community and actively engage with them. Such an approach to stewardship means that measuring abundance is never a fixed-sum game. It is not simply a redistribution of resources but a creation of something new. Generosity has a compounding effect, and we can build something together that we could never do separately. In the process, we move beyond a stewardship paradigm that simply asks us to pay our fair share. Instead, stewardship engages our passions, frees us from the power of money, deepens relationships, and opens our imaginations to a new way of seeing the world. Stewardship of finances as faith formation allows us to see human flourishing beyond just wealth to the flourishing of our lives as generous disciples as well as the flourishing of communities with which we are engaged to bring about the kingdom of God in the world.

Questions for Reflection

1. What is your earliest family memory of giving and volunteering?
2. Who have been some of your heroes and role models that reflect a generous life?
3. To what people and places do you feel a sense of gratitude?
4 What are the one or two life experiences that have shaped who you are today?
5. What is precious to you?
6. What values do you want to pass on to your family and friends?

Applications for Life Together

- Create opportunities for education and practice around debt management, budgeting, and general financial health. Consider how these practices connect to a life of faith and wholeness and how they might be lived out within the context of community.
- Consider how leaders might foster a sense of transparency around their own giving practices as well as the areas in which they hope to grow.
- Embrace more opportunities for telling the story of God's work in your congregation. If you do not have a robust system of thanking givers (of money, time, and other resources), consider implementing one.

4

Stewardship of Technology

Digital Gifts

ADAM J. COPELAND

It was a late spring that year, so my friends Paul and Ingrid, a young couple in their early thirties, decided to get out of the city and go for a drive. They ended up at a café in Stillwater, Minnesota, along the banks of the St. Croix River. They ordered cocktails and appetizers. All of a sudden, Paul collapsed. Employees and customers alike rushed over and lowered Paul's limp body to the floor. He was unconscious. His heart had stopped beating. Somebody called 911.

A nurse led chest compressions, and Ingrid administered mouth-to-mouth. Before too long, the paramedics arrived. As Ingrid puts it, the paramedics had all the tools they lacked— clear minds, oxygen, and an Automated External Defibrillator, or AED. All it took was one shock with the AED, and Paul was revived from sudden cardiac arrest. The paramedics whisked him off to the hospital, and a kind waitress drove Ingrid close behind. At the hospital, a highly trained medical team conducted surgery under bright lights with medicine's latest tools, installing an Implantable Cardioverter Defibrillator (ICD).

Paul has made a full recovery. Some two months later, Ingrid wrote a letter to the editor that appeared in the

Stillwater Gazette. She ended the letter by acknowledging it took some time "to articulate what we knew right away: in the midst of the sorrow and loss, the fear and pain, a certain grace found us in the women and men we had never before seen and may never see again." Indeed, without the quick thinking and kindness of the café's workers, the nurse and paramedics, and the entire medical team at the hospital, Paul likely would have died. His very life is now a testament to the gift of caring for strangers.[1]

One cannot tell the story of the day Paul's life was saved without noting the gifts of humanity. But that is not the full story. A human used a phone to call 911. The ambulance, with its horsepower, radios, and sirens, sped on the asphalt of Stillwater's roads. The electrodes of the AED sent a reading to the computer hidden in its machinery before it sent a 3,000-volt charge to Paul's chest in less than 0.001 of a second. And then Paul arrived at the hospital, where the forms of technology are too numerous to count.

Usually, discussion of technology in the church moves quickly to talk of computers, iPhones, and tablets, and then narrows even more to social-media tools like Facebook and Twitter. This chapter will certainly approach electronic gadgets and digital communication technologies, but I also seek to broaden the usual conversation. Since discussions of gifts are essential when discussing stewardship, I will anchor these reflections with the claim that technology is a gift. After all, in the hands of kind strangers and highly trained professionals, technology helped save Paul's life.

I once saw a news story about a West Coast coffee shop that offered a highly sought-after commodity: technology-free space. The coffee shop walls were lined with a metal that blocked cell phone signals. Customers were invited to use manual typewriters available at many tables. The only Internet connection offered was exceedingly slow—the dial-up speeds of the 1990s. The story appeared on April 1, and the next day I, like many others, was brought in on the joke. The coffee shop was a fake, a comedic ruse made up for laughs on April Fools' Day. But I, like thousands of other news consumers, didn't get the joke. I like to think that fact is due less to my naiveté than to my heart's longing. Something about the story, in an unexpected way, drew out truth: I long for a haven from technology and its effect on us.

What do we make of this inherent dissonance? On the one hand, I'm deeply aware of the gift of technology that helped save Paul's life. On the other hand, I pine for a world in which coffee shops offer a Sabbath, a space set apart from the incessant pings and prodding of email, Internet, and iWhatnot. This chapter explores that paradox and searches for a balance, a stewardship of the technology that both saves and destroys modern life.

The Gift of Technology

Like all in God's world, we can use the gift of technology for God's glory, for justice, for the care of one another, and for the nourishing of all creation. God, after all, is all about making things. The first pages of scripture remind us that God made light and darkness, sky and land, plants and trees, birds and cattle, and even humankind. And God called it "good," and "very good."

Michael Lindvall writes, "It ought to be clear God doesn't hate stuff." In fact, God might be called the great materialist. With Lindvall, I wonder if, in our kneejerk critique of consumerism, we might go too far in the other direction. "The problem," writes Lindvall, "is not so much that we like stuff too much; rather it's that we don't like it enough."[2] Writing off stuff is easy, but examining our relationship with stuff—whatever that stuff may be—is both more difficult and more important.

When the psalmist first sang, "The earth is the Lord's and all that is in it," there were no laptops, or automobiles, or "smart" bombs on the earth (Ps. 24:1). So we might be tempted to read Psalm 24 and its claims as a remnant of another time, a glimpse into a bygone age in which God's handiwork felt more real and closer to humanity's lived reality. But we cannot escape the truth that God creates. Without God, not only would computers not exist, we and all the world would not exist. God spoke creation into being, and we owe everything to God.

It is worth pausing to note how very countercultural this claim is, even for practicing Christians. So much of North American culture is based upon the notion that we create our own destiny. Blatantly false phrases like "self-made man," or even "self-made millionaire," infect our understanding of dependency. It's even a bragging right for technology startups to claim they began in someone's garage, bootstrapping their way to glory. But this type of language and values begins a sort of slippage. We think:

- Surely God gifted me with intellect, but I did make my own choices.
- Surely God supported me, but I did earn that raise myself.
- Surely God put me in the right place, but I did the hard work all on my own.

And it doesn't take too long journeying down this path until we have separated God's gifts from our own supposed accomplishments. But the truth is this: without God we would be nothing. God knit us and formed us, and in God we are wonderfully made (see Ps. 139). God gives life and breath to all things, for "in him we live and move and have our being" (Acts 17:28).

Several of the founding fathers were deists; they believed in a distant God who created the universe and then left it to run its course. Perhaps, for this reason, appeals to God's gifts rather than those of our own creation seem vaguely—or sometimes *directly*—un-American. The spirit of the country emphasizes worth based in individual accomplishment. But, as many pastors remind their congregations before collecting the offering, "Every good gift comes from God." We want to tell ourselves we made it, did it, built it, own it; but no matter what *it* is, we *possess* it only for a time to use for God's glory. Technology must be counted among the things—the creation—that belong to God. Because of God's goodness, we are graced with the gift of technology. God then calls us— *obliges* us—to give to others.

Employing "gift" language is a common practice in stewardship circles, one about which Charles Lane wisely cautions. Lane argues that referring to items, money, even technologies as gifts from God may suggest that they become ours alone, that a transfer of ownership has occurred between us and God.[3] Appreciating Lane's caution, I have come to welcome gift language when considered through the lens of relationship. Gifts connect the giver and the receiver. Theologian Miroslav Volf points out that no "thing," just by itself, is a gift. While stores we call "gift shops" exist, the items in them are not gifts, but things like any other that may become gifts when bought and given. Therefore, "a gift is a social relation, not an entity or an act itself. It is an event *between* people."[4]

As those who have received from God, we give to others because it is core to our identity as human. Volf writes, "To live in sync with who we truly are means to recognize that we are dependent on God for our very breath and are graced with many good things; it means to be grateful to the giver and attentive to the purpose for which the gifts are given."[5] For Volf, God is giver, not only so we enjoy God's gifts, but so we may also pass them on to others. The point is not that technology becomes more meaningful when given as a birthday present (though, perhaps it does), but that technology, like all gifts from God, is best understood in relationship. It pushes us to ask questions like: How does God call us to employ the gift of technology? How might technology support or hinder our call to love God and neighbor?

Technology Is Not Neutral

Every morning an alarm on my iPhone alerts me to the unfortunate reality that it's time to wake up. Then, two minutes later, a second alarm makes the point again. Every night before I go to bed I set these alarms with the flick of a finger. I rest easily knowing that my phone will wake me. Every once in a while, though, I forget to set my alarm. Or, on some Friday nights, I decide to let myself sleep in the next morning, and I opt not to set an alarm at all. Nine times out of ten, I still wake up at the same time I usually set my alarm. I'm not a teenager anymore. Sleeping in is hard work!

My morning routine may be familiar to you. Sometimes we say that our bodies are "programmed" to wake up at a certain time. And, for most of us, this time has to do with when we usually set our alarm clocks. But what do we mean by the word *program*? It implies forethought, organization, and quite often is used in conjunction with technology and coding. Indeed, "programmer" is a job title for many who work with computers or on the Internet. Even the simple act of setting an alarm each night has affected my habits and lifestyle. So, have I programmed myself, or has my phone alarm programmed me?

In casual conversation, I often hear the phrase "Technology is neutral." Usually, what people mean is that technology, much of it at least, is seemingly passive. And I suppose it's true that my phone just sits on my bedside table when the alarm goes off. It does not jump off the table and nudge me in my bed (though, surely, the day will come). Similarly, my phone requires that I set the alarm each night. And yet, as noted above, the act of setting that alarm has turned me into somebody programmed to wake up at a certain time. Even on days I fail to set the alarm, this so-called passive technology wakes me up because of my history using it.

Two aphorisms refute the notion that technology is neutral. One is born of media theorist Marshall McLuhan's thinking: "We become what we behold. We shape our tools and our tools shape us."[6] The other speaks of tools directly: "If all you have is a hammer, everything looks like a nail."[7] Both statements point to the fact our lives and actions, often without us even noticing, become shaped by the technologies around us. Hammers, alarm clocks, computers, potato mashers, even ice cream scoops can shape our living.

Rather than pretending technology is neutral, the faithful way to approach technology appreciates its power to form our lives. Even as we understand technology in relationship to God the Giver, we can also note how the decisions of human technology designers cause technology to shape us. Building awareness of the shaping nature of technology can help frame a way of life that forms us into disciples of Jesus Christ, primarily shaped and formed by God's word and witness.

What Are We Shaping?

While I enjoy talking with my in-laws on the phone—really, I do—I speak with them extremely rarely. Cell-phone technology plays a huge role in this disconnect. My wife, Megan, and I don't have a landline phone. So, when my in-laws call, they dial the number of Megan's iPhone. Megan always answers because, well, it's her phone. If we had a landline phone, from time to time I'd likely answer a call from my in-laws and speak to them before handing the phone over to Megan. Our decision not to have a landline phone, in a roundabout way, shapes my relationship with my in-laws.

Many have noticed how their cell phones seem to be shaping their lives in ways both subtle and substantial. I noticed recently that when I walk between buildings on campus, my first reaction when stepping out the door is not to look around and appreciate the beauty of God's creation, but to take my phone from my pocket and read my latest emails, or check Twitter, while walking. Reading a phone screen (or typing a text message) while walking is a special skill—not a personal spiritual gift—and I admit at times I have actually veered off the path. It turns out, however, that I'm not alone. In 2015, the National Safety Council added "distracted walking" to its annual safety report. They found that a majority of adult cell phone users have run into something or someone while using their device![8] Reflecting on this statistic, given the choice between a slightly delayed response to a tweet and walking into a tree, I now choose tree avoidance every time.

It's certainly tempting to wax cynical about cell-phone technology's effects on our lives. I sometimes get frustrated when colleagues break eye contact to check their latest text message vibrating on their Apple Watch, and I'm no fan of students texting during class, but when I get frustrated, I think back to a meme. A photo that went viral on social media is of a Philadelphia commuter train circa 1955. The image shows dozens of men sporting suits, ties, and hats headed to work on the crowded train. In seat after seat, each commuter is holding up a large, printed newspaper and reading silently. Nobody is speaking to others or even acknowledging another's existence. The caption reads, "All this technology is making us antisocial."

Today, a similar packed commuter car in Philadelphia will play host to dozens of people staring down at cell-phone screens, tablets, and e-book readers. We might deem these commuters similarly antisocial, except for the fact that many are using those devices to nurture relationships with others. Perhaps they are playing a word game with friends, or commenting on a friend's Facebook post, or texting prayers to a family member. Perhaps they are reading the *Philadelphia Inquirer*, only in app form. So, before we wrap ourselves in a warm blanket of contempt and reminisce about the good ol' days before cell phones, we would be wise to stop and reflect.

At their core, social-media platforms like Facebook, Twitter, Instagram, and others have to do with human relationships and how we engage with one another. Keith Anderson and Elizabeth Drescher have written a helpful book for digital leadership and Christian ministry. Early on, they remind readers that the point of using digital technologies and social media is not *how many* people hear your voice, but "about how you are connected in meaningful, personal ways with people across diverse networks."[9] Especially when it comes to ministry, digital practice "is networked and relational rather than broadcast and numerical."[10] This frame reflects my own practices, at least when it comes to my iPhone. Rarely a day goes by when I fail to send text messages to friends and family. I am also part of several text-message groups set up so that messages we send are received by a group of friends simultaneously. We use these groups for both fun, humorous messages—such as sending cartoon avatars of ourselves with messages to one another—as well as to support one another in difficult times.

In her book on the social lives of teens, researcher danah boyd [*sic*] describes how teenagers navigate digital life today. boyd points to the structured lives of teenagers who lack transportation options, and who are often restricted from hanging out with one another in person, often because of parents' fears for their safety. "While parental restrictions and pressures are often well intended, they obliterate unstructured time and unintentionally position teen sociality as abnormal," boyd writes.[11] Through her conversations with and observations of teenagers, boyd appreciates that their use of social media and digital devices may seem excessive to outsiders. It may appear that some teenagers are addicted to social media. boyd posits, though, that teenagers are simply using technology because of the restrictions we have put upon them. "Social media has become a place where teens can hold court. Their desire to connect, gossip, and hang out only makes sense in response to the highly organized and restricted lives teens lead," writes boyd.[12] If given the option, they would prefer socializing in person. Absent that possibility, they embrace the human desire to connect to one another using the technologies they have.

Long before Facebook, John Calvin wrote, "Man's nature, so to speak, is a perpetual factory of idols."[13] Time has borne out the wisdom of Calvin's description. Perhaps because of our propensity to create our own gods, the technologies we shape often have a particularly enchanting quality to them. It takes a lot of willpower not to answer a ringing phone. Indeed, movie theaters wrestle with how to deal with patrons who cannot go two hours without looking at their brightly lit phone screens, even if it's to text friends about the film or tweet a quick reaction to it. Craig Detweiler warns, "Idols serve our needs according to our schedule. When we call, they answer. They give us a false sense of being in control. But over time, the relationship reverses. We end up attending to their needs, centering our lives on their priorities and agendas. Most idols begin as good things."[14] It is possible to celebrate the gift of technology, and, at the same time, take care not to become so entranced by its glow that we lose perspective.

Thankfully, it does not take long to find examples of hope rooted in technology. For example, the seminary where I teach offers a Distributed Learning program that enables those who otherwise could not gain a theological degree a means by which to do so. I have a friend who, once a week, scrolls through his Facebook feed and offers prayers for those who appear. For him, Facebook updates have become a sort of spiritual practice. Personally, I appreciate the technological advancement of receiving a daily devotion in my email inbox early each morning, and having a Bible app on my phone. Though perhaps overblown, predictions concerning the possibilities of advanced, self-driving electric cars—reducing carbon pollution and auto crashes while also freeing time for other pursuits—seem, in my view, quite appealing. But, as with all technology, self-driving cars will shape our habits anew.

Technology and Jesus

When it comes to biblical interpretation, scripture speaks to some contemporary themes more clearly than others. In an article about preaching on the subject of money, Lance Pape suggests that even regarding money—a topic Jesus spoke about often—the church often takes the wrong approach to interpretation.[15] With Pape, I cringe at sermon series and Bible studies that promise to explain "the Bible's teaching on X." Whether "X" is sex, money, or the latest hot-button social issue, reading scripture as primarily an answer book for our burning questions is neither reasonable nor faithful.

Even so, it's not difficult to find preachers addressing technology in topic-based sermons and sermon series. Chris Ridgeway experienced it so often, he discerned a common formula employed in these sermons: begin with a family-dinner illustration; beautiful dinner is rudely interrupted by buzzing phone; pose indicting question about how technology is distancing us from one another; quote scripture; end with the call to Sabbath. But instead of rote preaching about technology, Ridgeway calls the church to "preach about *people* living in a technological world."[16]

Building upon a long line of biblical scholars and preachers, Lance Pape argues that the Gospels are not about ethical, high-minded concepts like virtue or even love. Instead, Pape argues, the Gospels are about Jesus the *person*. It's not as if we take this concept, *love*, and then look to Jesus as love's best role model. Instead, for Pape, "we know what true love is only when we encounter this unique and unsubstitutable identity, Jesus Christ."[17] The Gospels are about the person Jesus, not a concept—money, technology, power—but Jesus. In Jesus, we see God's own being. Further, this person, Jesus, lived in relationship with others, teaching in community, and basing his interactions on God's love for those whom he encountered. Attempts to detach Jesus from these relationships with others, or to read the Gospels as a cut-and-paste instruction manual, fall short.

To preach from the Gospels about technology, we can use Pape's reframed question. The point is not, "What did Jesus say about X?" After all, Jesus said *nothing* about iPhones, electric cars, and Bluetooth headsets. Instead, the question becomes, "What would it mean to ponder X in the presence of Jesus?" What would it mean to ponder *technology* in the presence of Jesus? God's people certainly will not agree on the answers, but approaching the question this way opens space for rich and varied conversation.

Conclusion

For two reasons, this chapter avoids instructions on how to steward specific technological platforms. First, one person's social-media oversharing is another person's authentic communication. In other words, faithful approaches to specific uses of technological tools are as diverse as God's people. Second, technology is changing at such a rapid pace that what seem like wise words in late 2016 may prove hopelessly naïve by 2020. And yet, I feel I must end by staking some broader claims.

Roger Willer suggests a way forward in a speculative article considering what existing social statements of the Evangelical Lutheran Church in America (ELCA) might say to what some philosophers call *posthumanism*, or the technologically enhanced condition of humanity beyond what is merely human. In sum, Willer argues that any use of technology be justified according to the universal imperative of love for God's creation. This is stated in an ELCA statement as the goal to "respect and promote the community of life with justice and wisdom."[18] In other words, our approach to stewarding technology must also align with our other stewardship efforts. It is not as if technology gives humanity a free pass. In fact, because of the very power of technology, we must even more carefully consider how we steward it in our life together. ELCA teaching argues, "The human vocation to be innovative stewards must be guided by the goal to respect and promote the earth's abundance for the sake of the community of life."[19] Willer ends his article with a speculative judgment that, with precautions, ELCA teachings may suggest an "openness to some of the intentions and outcomes" suggested by posthuman thinking. It is our vocation, then, to live as "innovative stewards" of God's creation, embracing the gift of technology while questioning its effects on the common good.[20]

Technology is an inescapable part of modern life. At times, we notice it clearly—the shriek of an alarm clock, the ring of an iPhone, or the jolt of a defibrillator—but most of what we think of as technology has become so enmeshed in our lives that we give it little notice. As I made my breakfast this morning, I did not stop to consider the electricity that runs my toaster, the grinder that readied my coffee beans, and certainly not the eyeglasses that helped me see my toast and coffee mug clearly. Embracing the stewardship of technology invites us to pause and notice these technological gifts. Noticing pushes us to remember God, from whom all blessings flow. It also calls us to ponder whether we are using those gifts for God's glory, for seeking justice, and for loving one another. God's gift of technology isn't neutral, but neither are we. Let's steward it with wisdom, love, and grace.

Questions for Reflection

1. In what ways does technology help you love and care for your neighbor?
2. Have any technologies become idols for you? How might they be reimagined in light of an awareness of God's gifts?
3. Are your daily practices with digital tools supporting your relationships with others and building up God's beloved community?
4. How is technology shaping you—positively and negatively—for discipleship, witness, and service?
5. Consider a particular technology. What would it mean to ponder it in the presence of Jesus?

Applications for Life Together

- As a congregation, or as part of a small group ministry, track your use of a particular technology for a day or a week. Invite discussion about how the technology connected you with others, supported your relationships, and helped you serve God. In what ways did it cultivate or hinder your pursuit of love, mercy, and justice?
- Embark on a technology (perhaps, specifically, a social media) fast or Sabbath. What did you notice? In what ways do you feel refreshed and/or disconnected? How might you seek to shift future practices?

5

Stewardship of Privilege

Toward the Stewardship of Incarnation

MARGARET P. AYMER

Years ago, a friend and I sat down to discuss societal privilege. At the time, I counseled him to use his privilege for good. And he has, in remarkable, concrete ways that will have lasting effects. That encounter inspired my initial thoughts about privilege and stewardship. Indeed, I was originally to write about "the stewardship of privilege." However, I have come to reject the suggestion that privilege be stewarded. Instead, I propose a different tack. I believe that Christian faith calls us to the stewardship of incarnation. Such stewardship serves as an ethical critique of (un)earned societal privilege. In making this proposal, I am challenging my own earlier advice. Back then, I called my friend to use his privilege for good. Today, I would call him to honor his and others' incarnation. For, in doing so, we unmask the sin of societally constructed privilege.

Incarnation and Privilege: Working Definitions

The word *incarnation* encompasses a wide semantic range. Within Christian circles, it points, primarily, to the Christ event. It names the *enfleshment* of God-with-us as Jesus of Nazareth. Here incarnation does not merely stand against the Docetic heresy that suggests Jesus only seemed human (1 John 4:2).[1] It also opposes the Marcionite heresy, divorcing Jesus from his Jewish moorings. Jesus' incarnation signals God's divine inbreaking into human particularity: body and culture, class and society, privilege and disadvantage. Through Jesus, God is with us as a first-century, Hellenized, Palestinian Jewish male, a wandering teacher and prophet. He eats particular foods (fish and grain, bread and wine). He is instructed by Jewish scriptures. He speaks Aramaic and Greek with a Galilean accent.

All human beings, similarly, live as incarnate beings. Incarnation here points to our shared experiences of enfleshment. Like Jesus, we also are born into human particularities: body and culture, class and society, privilege and disadvantage. These particularities may include our physical coloration; the shape and size of our bodies, hair, eyes; our physical strength; and other attributes, such as the shape and functionality of various biological organs and our limbs. However, our incarnation includes more than our bodies. Our culture, also, is part of our incarnation: all of our artistic expressions, our languages—spoken, felt, and gestured—our abilities for socially approved ways of interaction and learning. Even our God talk emerges from our incarnation. Our cultures, languages, traditions—as well as our bodies—inform our relationships with God. Consider how differently Christians celebrate Christmas globally, as just one example.

Incarnational variety should be understood as a gift of God to be celebrated. To this, Luke-Acts bears witness in the Pentecost narrative (Acts 2). The story is familiar: the descent of the Spirit on the disciples. The multinational Jewish population of Jerusalem (v. 5) gathers at the sound. But note: the Spirit's descent is multivocal and polyglottal. No one single incarnation—place of birth, for instance—is privileged. Instead, the Spirit proclaims the gospel in every present incarnational language. The work of the Spirit is not assimilation. No one tongue is upheld as ideal. Instead the Spirit's falling sanctifies the polyvalent incarnations of the crowd. God speaks through the incarnational plurality of God's people.[2]

Each of us is born an incarnational being. We are born, also, into a system of privileges reinforced by society. That system hierarchizes, or privileges, some incarnational realities over others. Male gender and male biology are privileged. So is a particular kind of lighter complexion; this usually does not include albinism. Some languages—English, for instance— are privileged over others; within the system, speakers of other languages can face discrimination or punishment.[3] Some forms of sexual attraction receive privilege also. Yet these traits, diversely expressed, are our birthright. Our families of origin, our abilities to learn in culturally acceptable ways, our accents and speech patterns in childhood, these are all parts of our incarnational inheritance.

These societal privileges based on incarnation have consequences. They affect access to needs: food, medicine, clothing, shelter, physical safety, the assumption of innocence, freedom of movement, education, and employment. These can also affect access to social voice. Privilege often determines whether protests against unfair treatment will be heard, believed, and addressed.

Let me stress here that our incarnational particularities are not inherently bad. Ballet and haka, for example, are both forms of cultural expression through movement. Each has its origins in a particular culture. Neither is inherently "better" or "worse" than the other. Similar arguments can be made for raga and reggae, or kente and calico. The problem is not the differences in culture. The incarnational diversity of human creativity is one of the blessings of God. However, systemic privilege forces these differences into hierarchical relationships. Incarnationally, we may cook a variety of foods. Systemically, some foods are privileged over others. Incarnationally, we may speak a variety of languages. Systemically, some language groups are privileged over others.

By *privilege*, here, I do not mean "preference." Included in privilege is the question of societal power, which reinforces preference with power structures. Thus, speakers of one incarnational language may find themselves silenced in schools. They may be systemically denied access to education, employment opportunities, housing, or commerce.[4] Persons incarnated into a non-privileged phenotype (whether by gender, color, physical ability, or other incarnation) may find themselves facing social or systemic discrimination because of their phenotype.[5]

Privilege can thus be conceptualized as socially created hierarchies that normalize and protect particular human incarnations through soft or hard forms of social control (e.g., hiring preference, police protection). Within this system, other human incarnations are treated as non-normative, perhaps even deviant, and face soft and hard forms of social violence (e.g., discrimination, criminalization).

Understood thus, privilege is revealed to be a form of sin. It elevates some forms of human incarnation over others. In so doing, it invalidates the Golden Rule (Luke 6:31) and the second great commandment (Matt. 22:39; Mark 12:31; Luke 10:27; Lev. 19:18). If we understand stewardship as carefully tending the "manifold grace of God" (1 Pet. 4:10), we cannot then propose a stewardship of privilege. We must, instead, consider a stewardship of incarnation. This kind of stewardship must carefully tend our incarnations: bodies, families, languages, and cultures.

Privilege as Cultural: A Call to Prophetic Challenge

Here, we must pause. For, if we are honest, cultures encode and legitimate structures of privilege. Consider the household codes of Ephesians 6 and other parts of the New Testament. In the midst of a call to live as "imitators of God," the writer inserts household codes. These concretize privileges for freeborn adult men, baptizing them as holy. The damage of these household codes continues among descendants of slaves, and abused women and children. This, then, is the tension. Being stewards of incarnation, including of culture, does not mean ignoring systemic privilege. Such privilege bears false witness against God and often causes irreparable harm. Instead, the stewardship of incarnation must be prophetic. It must name as unethical those structures of privilege embedded within cultures. At the same time, stewardship of incarnation cannot dismiss an entire culture as evil simply on the basis of its embedded structures of privilege. Rather, our call as stewards is to unearth cultural moments that can serve as alternatives, models for what culture could be. These moments may, then, be invoked in a prophetic challenge against the sin of privilege.

A word of caution must be spoken here. Persons from cultures that are systemically privileged—global, Northern, Western, Christian—often have an easier time identifying the embedded systemic privileges in every culture except their own. Standing with those who name a particular incarnational oppression can be ethical and good. Naming various practices, like genital mutilation, as acts of biologically determined systemic oppression can be prophetic. Still, we who come from privileged cultures must be cautious. We have not yet begun to name or to challenge our own systemic privileges. Yet we often have the temerity to name others' cultural practices as sin. If we are to live into a stewardship of incarnation, our primary stance must be humility. Else we shall repeat the ethnocentrism and racism of our forebears. Not every unfamiliar cultural norm is oppressive. Not every unfamiliar practice is sinful.

The Stewardship of Incarnation: Norms

As any pastor, teacher, or parent knows, the job description never fully describes the job. So it is with stewardship. What follows is a series of four norms. These norms are not proposed as a checklist of appropriate action. Stewardship is not so much a series of actions as an orientation, a commitment to nurture the gracious gifts of God. And so, these norms describe orientations. Adopting these norms—or orientations—will help to facilitate the stewardship of incarnation.

Kenosis

The first of these norms seems counterintuitive. It derives from the Christ hymn of Philippians 2. In it, Paul calls the Philippians to imitate Christ who "emptied himself / taking the form of a slave" (Phil. 2:7a). Theologians call this act of self-emptying *kenosis*. Misused, *kenosis* can be oppressive. One can appeal to it to justify abandoning one's incarnation in favor of a system of privilege. In this logic, women might abandon their cries to be recognized in their full humanity. They might "empty themselves" in favor of a society that privileges men. However, this is a misapplication of Philippians 2. As Paul records the *kenotic* event, Christ Jesus, "though he was in the form of God, / did not regard equality with God / as something to be exploited" (v. 6). As J. Kameron Carter has noted, the *kenosis* of the Christ is a self-emptying of privilege, not of incarnation.[6] Christ abandons privilege in favor of incarnation. Christ abandons divine form in favor of human particularity—embodiment, language, culture. Only through this *kenosis* does Christ become the ultimate steward of incarnation.

Kenosis thus understood invalidates privilege, preventing further oppression of those already societally devalued. *Kenosis* challenges those whose incarnations are privileged, who are treated by society as though they were god-like. To follow the Christ is to engage in *kenosis*. As imitators of Christ, we are called to empty ourselves of our privilege and to enter fully into our incarnate particularities. In that incarnation, we encounter the Holy. For, as we have seen, the Spirit of God moves through, not in spite of, our incarnation.

Interdependence—*Ubuntu*

The surprising truth about *kenosis* is that it does not lead to our disappearance. Instead, *kenosis*, rightly understood, leads to interdependence. My colleague Carolyn Helsel puts it this way: when we engage in the joyful discipline of *kenosis*, we

become able "to receive knowledge of ourselves from others
. . . we turn to one another and we receive ourselves, uniting ourselves to others out of the unity with God that Christ
enabled."[7] This too is a norm of the stewardship of incarnation. To understand this more concretely, we turn once more
to Paul. His metaphor of the church as the body of Christ
points toward interdependence. The body, writes Paul,
requires each of its members to function interdependently.
Therefore, the body cannot reject any member as unneces-
sary or dispensable.

Paul's metaphor provided a helpful corrective to a Corin-
thian community steeped in the privilege structure of the
Roman Empire. However, Paul veers closely toward a stewardship of privilege rather than of incarnation. His metaphor
continues with these words:

> On the contrary, the members of the body that seem
> to be weaker are indispensable, and those members
> of the body that we think less honorable we clothe
> with greater honor, and our less respectable mem-
> bers are treated with greater respect; whereas our
> more respectable members do not need this. (1 Cor.
> 12:22–24)

Paul seems to imply a challenge to the hierarchical structures of his society. However, his metaphor can also reinforce
them. He can be read as challenging only the *unjust* use of
one's societal privilege. If, however, societal privileging of
particular incarnations is sinful, then Paul's metaphor moves
us only part of the way.

A different, but related, metaphor emerges from the
Nguni Bantu languages of southern Africa: *ubuntu*. Translated roughly, "I am because you are," the metaphor pushes
beyond the Pauline notion of more and less honored members of the body, a re-inscription of privilege. It points to
a more radical interdependence, interdependence reliant
simply on the fact of incarnation. To quote Archbishop Desmond Tutu:

> A person with Ubuntu is open and available to others, affirming of others, does not feel personally threatened that others are able or good, for he or she has a proper self-assurance that comes from knowing that he or she belongs in the greater whole and is diminished when others are humiliated or diminished, when others are tortured or oppressed.[8]

For stewards of incarnation, *ubuntu* hints to a greater truth. Our individual incarnations do not have value only in themselves. They are part of a larger, radically diverse whole. That creative whole is diminished when anyone's incarnation is devalued. Conversely, each of our incarnations, and the creation as a whole, depends on the fullness of everyone else's incarnation. *Ubuntu* is necessarily anti-hierarchical. It requires recognition of the other's full incarnation as a gift and a co-equal source of God's grace.

Anti-Idolatry

Both *kenosis* and *ubuntu* concern our self-understanding as incarnate beings. The former helps us to see who we are. The latter helps us to recognize ourselves in relationship to others. We begin to see ourselves as part of a deeply interdependent, beautifully and radically diverse web of being.

A third norm of the stewardship of incarnation shifts our focus to those societal privileges that we have already named sin. Here, the Revelation to John serves as a helpful conversation partner. In Revelation 13, the seer of Patmos describes an often-misunderstood apocalyptic scene. After revealing not only the dragon but also two beasts—one from the sea and one from the land—the seer tells of the worship of the first beast. The people gather around it, shouting, "Who is like the beast, and who can fight against it?" (Rev. 13:4).

Generations of Christian theologians have tried to connect this beast with a person, a "whom." However, I contend that John here intends the beast to represent a "what." For John, the evil is not simply the beast—"Nero Caesar," as the alternatively attested numbers of 666 and 616 would seem to indicate. The evil for John is the *worship* of the beast. John's contention here is the misplacement of worship, the worship, not only of a person, but of an entire sinful system of privilege and power represented by that person. Power is vested in the system, and in the one representing the system. The system, identified as satanic, then metes out power to those who support it, and who cause others to do the same. Thus, the beast from the land has power only as a client of the beast from the sea who, in turn, serves the dragon.

John's larger point, often overlooked in the fantastical imagery of apocalypse, is a firm stance against idolatry. Here, idolatry should not be primarily understood as a stance against other cultures' god talk. Idolatry, for the seer, is the worship of Rome as the ultimate source of power and truth. For stewards of incarnation, this stance against idolatry follows self-emptying of societal privilege and recognition of *ubuntu* interdependence. These two preceding norms reveal societal systems of privilege for what they are: forms of idolatry. Worship, in this case, may not involve the building of physical temples. However, insofar as systems of privilege are considered unassailable ("who is like the beast and who can fight against it"), they lean in the direction of supplanting the role of God for Christians. This is a form of idolatry.

As with Rome, the object of worship here is not a "who" but a "what." In this case, it is systemic privileges based on incarnational traits. These systemic privileges have names such as racism, sexism, classism, heterosexism, and so on. Within these systems, no individual persons are the focus of adoration. However, the unassailability of these systems nevertheless creates forms of worship, especially in those whose incarnations are not privileged. Take, for instance, white racism as one of the largest of these systems. Those whose incarnations are not privileged by that system frequently feel pressured to forms of self-sacrifice that include skin bleaching, hair straightening and lightening, and even forms of surgery.[9] These human sacrifices to the seemingly unassailable God of the white incarnational norm can appear self-inflicted.

However, once one engages in *kenosis* from white incarnational privilege, one begins to feel the harm that the devaluation of one incarnation causes to all incarnations. This in turn throws the beast and its worship into sharp focus. And, in turn, seeing the beast—these systems of privilege—as it is worshiped provokes a rejection of idolatry.

Similar realizations attend to other systemic incarnational privileges—gender, culture, language, embodiedness, sexual attraction, and the like. To each of these beasts, a kind of worship is paid. The seeming unassailability of these beasts calls forth, from those who are not thus privileged, forms of sacrifice. Language and accent are abandoned or hidden. The idealized gender norm, unattainable even for most born into male bodies, is mimicked by some and appeased by other devalued gendered incarnations. The pattern repeats itself for other devalued incarnations. Meanwhile, those who refuse to worship these beasts, just as in Revelation, face penalties: economic, social, even mortal.

A caution is necessary here. I have intentionally named anti-idolatry as the norm, rather than the more Protestant "iconoclasm." Insofar as icons are models and guides for the stewardship of incarnation, they can do much good. Here, I am thinking of lives well lived: whether ancients, like Gregory of Nyssa; or more recent models, like Desmond Tutu, Barbara Jordan, Dolores Huerta, and Grace Lee Boggs. We all need these kinds of iconic guides. Icons are not idols. They do not take the place of God. Instead, they demonstrate the practice of the stewardship of incarnation in particular times and places.

Solidarity

When one engages in *kenosis* and *ubuntu*, idolatry is not the only revelation. Revealed also is the harm that non-privileged incarnations face because of the sin of privilege. From this comes forth a call for solidarity. Within the Christian witness, this call takes two forms. First, stewards are called to meet the needs of those hurt by systems of privilege. Jesus proclaims this call in the parable of the final judgment (Matt. 25:31–40). Those whom Jesus praises and accepts in this parable have stood in solidarity with the hungry, thirsty, naked, sick, imprisoned, and estranged. These states of distress would have accompanied those whose incarnations Rome devalued. Similar themes attend in the Matthean and Lukean Beatitudes; and the letter of James (Matt. 5:1–12; Luke 6:20–26; Jas. 2).

This first form of solidarity is important. It addresses hurts caused by systemic privilege. It calls for restorative justice, and it highlights those who would normally be devalued. At the same time, like the body imagery of Paul, these measures by themselves risk turning into a kind of stewardship of privilege. That is, they risk making systemic privilege less toxic and more bearable without changing the system.

Thus, for stewards of incarnation, solidarity must go further. A preliminary example of this is found in Acts 6:1–7. In this narrative, a group within the Christian community of Jerusalem claims that it is being neglected. The charge is that of privilege. One cultural group—those Luke calls "Hebrews"—is being favored over another, those Luke calls "Hellenists." The response of the apostles is not merely to alleviate the harm. They call for the appointment of leaders from the devalued group to change the status quo. This kind of solidarity is necessarily preliminary. Those injured were women; however, those appointed to leadership were all men. Thus the systemic privileging of culture was addressed, but not of gender. Nevertheless, Acts 6 models solidarity in a different way from the examples of the Gospels and James above. Here, solidarity means changing structures. It means not only realizing one's interdependence with another but also empowering that other to lead. In Acts, it means inviting Hellenists to lead the church. And this, in turn, means living into *kenosis*, as those with power empty themselves on behalf of those who have been systemically disempowered.

Joseph Barnabas of Cyprus is another model for this second kind of solidarity. His story bridges the original Galilean followers of Jesus and the Hellenists in Acts 6. Likewise, his cultural location bridges these two groups. Born in Cyprus, he is an outsider to the Palestinian-born in-group of the early church leadership (Acts 4:36). Yet his Jewish name and heritage (a Levite) separate him from the culturally Greek leaders of Acts 6. His incarnation, as a Levite, grants him some societal privilege. Further, he owns property. He enters the story of Acts when, in enacted *kenosis*, he sells his property to help advance the church (Acts 4:37). Later, Luke tells of Barnabas vouching for the newly converted Saul of Tarsus (Acts 9:27). This same Barnabas, having been sent to Antioch by the church, calls Saul into leadership, serving perhaps as a mentor for the younger believer (Acts 11:19–26).

Barnabas points to solidarity as mentorship and capacity building. These are also forms of empowerment. They require long-term, ongoing commitment and the willingness to be displaced. Barnabas consistently stewards incarnation through this less visible but equally critical role. In Luke's telling, he not only empowers the church, he helps to mentor into full voice its most important leader of the first century. Indeed, it is possible that his break with Paul was also around this matter of mentoring. His willingness to attend to the young, imperfect Mark contrasted with Paul's impatience (Acts 15:36–39). Barnabas, ever the mentor, stays with Mark. One might imagine he understands that the movement cannot rest on Paul's shoulders alone. There must be others to take his place, and someone must help them to grow into their incarnations also.

Certainly, one may argue that this also is a kind of stewardship of privilege. Barnabas, the more privileged, uses his position to mentor those without power. However, capacity building does not always have, as its end, the amelioration of the injustices of a system. Capacity building, the kind of empowerment and mentorship that Barnabas does, can also be a response to the *kenosis* of privilege, to interdependence, and to anti-idolatry. In the case of Barnabas, we see all of these. He empties himself, consistently giving away at least some of his privilege, whether his property (Acts 4), or his solo authority (Acts 11). He recognizes and stewards the incarnation of

Saul of Tarsus, both in Jerusalem and in Antioch. He refuses systemic idolatry within the church by sharing his leadership, and outside of the church by resisting those who would have made him Zeus (Acts 14). He does this, not to alleviate a system, but to help create one, a system standing in prophetic opposition to Rome. Like others I have mentioned, Barnabas is an iconic figure, not an idol to be worshiped. He points to a way of being a steward of not only one's property but also incarnation.

For the Healing of the Nations

In the third chapter of Genesis, Cain famously asks God, "Am I my brother's keeper?" A steward of incarnation would have to respond, "Yes, we all are." But what does that imply for the goal, the *telos,* of this kind of stewardship? This kind of stewardship points to the dismantling of the curses of systemic privilege. Most of the time, we consider systemic privilege's impact on those whose incarnations are devalued. However, consider the obverse. In the United States, "whiteness" has been systemically privileged, a norm against which all other phenotypical and cultural incarnations are devalued. However, "whiteness" is not actually an incarnation. Those deemed "white" vary significantly in phenotypic expression. Some of those deemed "not white" proceed to "pass for white." Others considered "white" are easily judged and devalued as "nonwhite" for seeming to violate norms of the system.[10] The system is porous. Moreover, "whiteness" as a cultural incarnation represents a dismantling and discarding of incarnational diversity and richness.

Hidden by this pall of whiteness are the multilingual and multivalent cultures of Europe and other parts of the world. In their place stands a manufactured substance, somewhat palatable, that, like "American cheese," is processed, possibly edible, but in no way a true reflection of incarnation. The richness of the varieties of cultures, languages, phenotypes, and other incarnational expressions are lost. They too have been sacrificed to the beast of privilege. In this way, privilege hurts, not only those whose incarnations are devalued, but those whose are overvalued or homogenized for the sake of a larger system. In the name of the false promise of unity, the system makes impossible interdependence. That is, privilege destroys all incarnational diversity, not simply those forms that are devalued. To those living under this pall, separated from both others' incarnations and their own, stewardship of incarnation issues invitations to *kenosis*. The invitation is the same as it is to those with any privilege: an invitation, not to stewardship, but to self-emptying. Only when that privilege is laid down can we see the other, name the idolatry, and move toward solidarity.

The invitation is not merely for those with white privilege. As I have noted all along, all systems of privilege share some of these same markers. And many persons may live with both privileged and devalued aspects of their incarnation. Moreover, all of us learn to imitate the privileging structures around us. Shanell Smith's work on "Woman Babylon" (Rev. 18) underscores this. We all internalize privilege. We all mimic the beast and wonder who can fight against it. And often we do so quite un-self-consciously. Smith calls us to "ambi*veil*ance," to realizing the ways in which we all participate in the sinful structures of privilege that disempower and devalue others.[11]

In truth, this kind of stewardship is like weeding a garden. The work will be ongoing. The journey will be cyclical. Solidarity will reveal new privileges of which we need to be emptied in order to become fully incarnate. The work will be imperfect. We will never fully get it right. But the stewardship of incarnation is not an exam; it is ultimately a spiritual discipline. Its end: to live more fully as ourselves, created in the diverse and multivalent image of the God who chose to become fully, particularly, wonderfully incarnate.

Questions for Reflection

1. Where might systems of privilege be playing out in your congregation or community? Who might help you understand them more fully?

2. How does your congregation understand its relationship to the broader community in terms of systems of privilege and oppression?

3. This kind of stewardship is an ongoing, cyclical process. It's imperfect work, and yet when embraced, can become a spiritual discipline. When have you experienced movement toward a stewardship of incarnation? When have you noted times of failure? What might support this ongoing work?

Applications for Life Together

- Consider offering education series on various systems of injustice, either affecting people in your community or around the world.

- Seek out opportunities for service that provide an element of education and/or accompaniment around issues of justice. If education is not provided by your service site or organization, consider providing pre-education about the issue(s) you will be engaging (e.g., hunger, homelessness, poverty, racism). Better yet, invite someone who has experienced these issues/systems of injustice firsthand to share with you.

6

Stewardship of Spirit

Stewarding Spiritual Gifts

DAVID GAMBRELL

I had a dream one night—a type that will surely be familiar to anyone who has ever been a pastor, gone on a job interview, or even just attended middle school. In the dream I am visiting an unfamiliar church and having trouble navigating various books and bulletin inserts. Then I hear someone call my name. I am summoned to the front of the room and, to my great surprise, introduced as the preacher for the day. Sure enough, there's my name in the order of worship. I look out at the congregation and see a "who's who" of familiar faces—former professors, respected mentors, and other luminaries—all watching with great expectation. I look down at my empty hands—no sermon. And then I realize what I'm wearing—no robe, no stole, not even a jacket and tie—only tattered old khakis and an undershirt.

Naturally at that point I woke up in a cold sweat and gave thanks that it was only a dream. But I also knew immediately what I *should* have said and done. I should have said, "Grace and peace, people of God. My name is David, and I am baptized. I have no words for you but the good news of Jesus Christ. I have nothing to boast about but the grace of God, and that's more than enough for me. I have nothing to offer you today but the gifts of the Holy Spirit, poured out in abundance on us in baptism. And I am clothed in the only garment that matters, the righteousness of Christ my Savior." I should have remembered my baptism.

Remembering Your Baptism

We sometimes give keepsakes to help a person remember the day of his or her baptism—a book or a seashell, perhaps, a cross or a candle. These can be valuable, tangible ways of remembering our baptism. The most important gift we receive in baptism, however, is a little harder to grasp. It is a gift from God: the gift of the Holy Spirit, who will bless and keep *us* all the days of our lives. God pours out the Holy Spirit upon us, anointing us with the spiritual gifts we need to follow Jesus in faith and faithfulness. God's Spirit flows down like water to fill our lives with blessing.

The prophets of the Old Testament frequently spoke of the Spirit in this way. Isaiah gave God's benediction: "I will pour out my spirit upon your descendants, / and my blessing on your offspring" (Isa. 44:3). Through Ezekiel, God announced that the day would come "when I pour out my spirit upon the house of Israel" (Ezek. 39:29). Speaking to Joel, the Lord extended the promise: "I will pour out my spirit on all flesh" (Joel 2:28).

New Testament voices continued the theme, connecting the outpouring of the Holy Spirit with baptism. As Peter said (in the original Pentecost sermon), "'Repent, and be baptized every one of you in the name of Jesus Christ so that your sins may be forgiven; and you will receive the gift of the Holy Spirit'" (Acts 2:38). Paul used strong baptismal imagery to describe the gift of the Spirit in his letter to the church at Rome: "God's love has been poured into our hearts through the Holy Spirit that has been given to us" (Rom. 5:5). The epistle to Titus says that we receive God's gift of salvation "through the water of rebirth and renewal by the Holy Spirit," the same Spirit God "poured out on us richly through Jesus Christ our Savior" (Titus 3:5–6).

Drawing on these and other biblical accounts of baptism, the 1982 World Council of Churches statement on *Baptism, Eucharist, and Ministry* explains:

> God bestows upon all baptized persons the anointing and the promise of the Holy Spirit, marks them with a seal and implants in their hearts the first installment of their inheritance as sons and daughters of God. The Holy Spirit nurtures the life of faith in their hearts until the final deliverance when they will enter into its full possession, to the praise of the glory of God.[1]

Through the gifts and promise of the Spirit, bestowed in baptism, we are claimed as beloved children of God and equipped with the spiritual gifts we will need to love and serve the Lord.

For this reason, the laying on of hands in baptism is often accompanied by this litany of spiritual gifts, drawn from the prophet Isaiah (Isa. 11:2–3):

O Lord, uphold *(Name)* by your Holy Spirit.
Give *him/her* the spirit of wisdom and understanding,
the spirit of counsel and might,
the spirit of knowledge and the fear of the Lord,
the spirit of joy in your presence,
both now and forever.[2]

Among other things, remembering your baptism means remembering these gifts of the Spirit that are poured out so generously upon us by the God of all grace. We give thanks that God has called and equipped us to be people of insight, compassion, discernment, strength, intelligence, awe, and gladness—all through the power of the Holy Spirit at work in us.

Improving Your Baptism?

There is a phrase in the Westminster Larger Catechism that always sounded odd to me, even shockingly un-Reformed. Question 167 asks, "How is our Baptism to be improved by us?" How preposterous to presume that we might improve on what God has done in our baptism! And isn't God's grace sufficient for us? Are we not justified and sanctified by God's free grace alone? (Hint: see Questions 70 and 75.)

I began to suspect that the word "improve" had a different meaning in the seventeenth century when this catechism was composed. Sure enough, the trusty *Oxford English Dictionary* reveals that the word's range of meaning once included: "to make one's profit (of), to avail oneself (of) by using to one's profit," and "to turn (a thing) to profit or good account, to employ to advantage."[3] This makes more sense. We are called to make good use of the gifts God has given to us in baptism—in other words, to be good stewards of these spiritual gifts.

The answer provided in the Larger Catechism is lengthy (naturally) and requires some unpacking, but it is well worth reading in full:

> The needful but much neglected duty of improving our Baptism, is to be performed by us all our life long, especially in the time of temptation, and when we are present at the administration of it to others, by serious and thankful consideration of the nature of it and of the ends for which Christ instituted it, the privileges and benefits conferred and sealed thereby, and our solemn vow made therein; by being humbled for our sinful defilement, our falling short of, and walking contrary to, the grace of Baptism and our engagements; by growing up to assurance of pardon of sin, and of all other blessings sealed to us in that sacrament; by drawing strength from the death and resurrection of Christ, into whom we are baptized, for the mortifying of sin, and quickening of grace; and

by endeavoring to live by faith, to have our conversation in holiness and righteousness, as those that have
therein given up their names to Christ, and to walk in
brotherly love, as being baptized by the same Spirit
into one body.[4]

With its timeless wisdom, this centuries-old instruction
in Christian life encourages us to remember our baptism
throughout the days of our lives—particularly in times of
trouble; when we celebrate the baptism of others; and by regular reflection on the meaning, blessings, and promises of our
own baptism. It explains that the baptized life is one in which
we regularly confess our sin and trust in God's mercy, rely
on the strength of our crucified and risen Savior, and seek to
live as redeemed people, fully alive to God in Jesus Christ. As
people of new birth by water and the Spirit, we find our true
identity in Jesus' name and a true community in the church
that is Christ's body.

The catechism's answer to this question seems, furthermore, to call for or assume certain spiritual disciplines or habits of Christian life—practices of faith and faithfulness that
will help us to avail ourselves of the gift of our baptism. Such
disciplines might include, but are not certainly limited to:

- prayer ("in the time of temptation");
- participation in public worship ("when we are present
  at the administration of [baptism] to others");
- gratitude ("serious and thankful consideration of the
  nature of [baptism]");
- self-examination ("being humbled for our sinful
  defilement" and "growing up to assurance of pardon
  of sin");
- self-emptying ("drawing strength from the death and
  resurrection of Christ, into whom we are baptized,
  for the mortifying of sin, and quickening of grace");
- self-discipline ("endeavoring to live by faith, to have
  our conversation in holiness and righteousness");

- self-offering ("as those that have therein given up their names to Christ"); and
- fellowship in the community of faith ("to walk in brotherly love, as being baptized by the same Spirit into one body").[5]

As the catechism demonstrates, these classic spiritual disciplines flow from the water of baptism and help us to nurture a life in the Spirit.

Varieties of Gifts

What does a life in the Spirit look like? Unfortunately, many of us have inherited a rather narrow view of Christian spirituality, along with unhelpful stereotypes about "spiritual people." We may believe that a "real spiritual person" is never found without her dog-eared, leather-bound Bible, illuminated with a neon highlighter and fat with bookmarks; or that he drops to his knees and folds his hands three times a day, praying in perfect King James English; or that she avails herself of every opportunity for a silent retreat, labyrinth walk, and guided meditation; or that he keeps a perfect Lenten fast fifty-two weeks a year, wearing a suit of camel's hair and eating only locusts.

These are caricatures, of course, exaggerations and distortions drawn from venerable and salutary spiritual practices—devotional reading, daily prayer, contemplation, simplicity of life—that I do not disparage or dismiss. Yet these caricatures reflect the unrealistic ideals that persist in our imaginations and sabotage our spiritual practices. Just as televised singing competitions can send the message that music making is best left to the professionals and virtuosos, these images of "spiritual superstars" become false idols for us. They lead us to think that our own spiritual lives are hopelessly inadequate, that our own spiritual practices will never measure up or amount to anything in the eyes of God. They give us an excuse to abandon spiritual disciplines before ever really giving them a chance—supposing that such gifts have been granted only to the "anointed few."

The truth is that we are *all* anointed with the Holy Spirit in our baptism. We are all called to practice the faith into which we are baptized, using the spiritual gifts God has poured out in our lives. As the apostle Paul wrote to the church in Corinth, "Now there are varieties of gifts, but the same Spirit; and there are varieties of services, but the same Lord; and there are varieties of activities, but it is the same God who activates all of them in everyone. To each is given the manifestation of the Spirit for the common good" (1 Cor. 12:4–7). To paraphrase: there is one Lord, one God, one Spirit; but there is not just one kind of spiritual person. Rather, there are varieties of gifts, services, and activities in the body of Christ, all of which are needed for the sake of the whole, all of which must work together for the common good.

Like the early Christians in Corinth, we may clothe certain types of spiritual gifts with greater honor and respect, ignoring or devaluing others. We may distance or disassociate ourselves from other members of the body, believing that our (or their) particular gifts and blessings are of inferior quality and lesser use, or just don't belong. Becoming better stewards of our spiritual gifts will require, among other things, recognizing the rich diversity of gifts that are found in the body of Christ and the great value of the various gifts God has given to each of us. This too flows from the gift and calling of our baptism, as Paul proclaimed: "For just as the body is one and has many members, and all the members of the body, though many, are one body, so it is with Christ. For in the one Spirit we were all baptized into one body" (vv. 12–13).

Loving God, Loving Neighbor

Just as there are varieties of spiritual gifts, there are many and various ways to catalogue or conceptualize them—from well-respected personality inventories to informal, online quizzes that promise to pinpoint a person's spiritual type or preference. One should approach such instruments (especially the latter!) with a degree of caution or suspicion, particularly insofar as they may present false dichotomies, perpetuate stereotypes about spiritual experience, force people into artificial boxes, or even foster divisions within the body. God's creative Spirit, poured out upon and among the people of God, transcends boundaries and defies categorization.

Nevertheless, a thoughtful typology or survey can be very helpful in illuminating those facets of Christian faith and life we may fail to acknowledge or understand as authentic spiritual gifts. Glimpsing the multiple dimensions and expressions of spirituality can open us to new awareness of the presence and power of God in our lives. Considering the great array of spiritual types can assist us in discerning and claiming our own undiscovered gifts, or in recognizing and drawing out the hidden gifts of others.

In that spirit, I propose a fresh reading of Mark 12—not as yet another spiritual inventory, but as an invitation to the fullness and wholeness of life in the Spirit. You remember the story: religious experts decide to give Jesus a quiz of their own, challenging him to name the first and greatest commandment: "Jesus answered, 'The first is, "Hear, O Israel: the Lord our God, the Lord is one; you shall love the Lord your God with all your heart, and with all your soul, and with all your mind, and with all your strength"'" (Mark 12:29–30). Then Jesus goes for extra credit, adding: "The second is this, 'You shall love your neighbor as yourself.' There is no other commandment greater than these" (v. 31).

Citing the ancient *Shema* or "Great Commandment" (Deut. 6:4–5) alongside an encapsulation of Jewish ethical teaching (see Lev. 19:18), Jesus offers a perfect summary of the way of life to which God calls us. We are called to love and serve God with our hearts—in love, compassion, and care; souls—with imagination, connection, and creativity; minds—through our intelligence, knowledge, and wisdom; and strength—by our energy, activity, and will.[6] Furthermore, the juxtaposition of God and neighbor in this double commandment suggests that a full and authentic spiritual life takes place in both the interior/personal (loving God) and exterior/public spheres (loving neighbor) of our lives.

There are two caveats I must make in using this passage as a description of spiritual life. First, I don't believe it was Jesus' intent (or that of the *Torah*) to establish a spiritual typology or to distinguish between various ways of loving God. Rather, the focus of these Great Commandments is that we are called to love and serve God with *all* that we have and *all* that we are, *all* the gifts we have been given. Indeed, this is consistent with the less compartmentalized, more organic and holistic understanding of spiritual gifts I have advocated. Second, I realize that the embodied metaphors of "heart," "soul," "mind," and "strength" conveyed somewhat different meanings in Hebrew and Greek, not equivalent to our contemporary associations, nor universally held among the cultures of the world.

These two disclaimers aside, there are also two significant strengths that come from a spirituality rooted in this double commandment. First, the call to *love* God and neighbor helps us understand that spiritual disciplines are gifts of love, not acts of obligation. Too often, we experience spiritual practices as religious homework or pious chores. Rather, they are meant to be a way of loving the one who first loved us (1 John 4:19) and loving one another as Jesus loves (John 13:34). Second, the aforementioned juxtaposition of God and neighbor reveals the double gift of life in the Spirit: as we draw near to God in prayer, we find ourselves drawn closer to our neighbors; and as we reach out to our neighbors with love, we experience God reaching out with love for us.

Heart, Soul, Mind, and Strength

As a way of fleshing out what I have in mind, I will offer a few examples of spiritual disciplines and practices under four headings: heart, soul, mind, and strength. Each set of examples is divided into two subsections: "loving God" and "loving neighbor." I present these without much explanation or elaboration, as there are numerous excellent resources for unpacking and exploring each of these spiritual practices and discovering countless others.[7]

Gifts of the Heart

To love God with your heart is to cherish the gift of personal relationship with the Creator. Examples of spiritual practices might include: celebration and gratitude for God's grace; self-examination and confession as a way of seeking right relationship with God; dedicating one's time, talents, and gifts to God through self-offering and service.

To love your neighbor with your heart is to desire full and abundant life for others. Examples of spiritual practices might include: evangelism and outreach with the good news of the gospel; acts of compassion and care for those who are hungry, thirsty, strangers, naked, sick, or in prison; offering hospitality to friends, neighbors, travelers, or refugees.

Gifts of the Soul

To love God with your soul is to long for deeper communion with the mystery of the divine. Examples of spiritual practices might include: contemplative prayer, centering prayer, breath prayer, or some other form of attentiveness to the presence of God; stillness, solitude, silent retreat, or Sabbath-keeping (as a way to rest in God's presence); journaling or everyday conversation with God in prayer.

To love your neighbor with your soul is to foster closer connections with others. Examples of spiritual practices might include: the exercise of pastoral care, extending the grace of Christ to those who are in need of healing, hope, consolation, or support; participating in a covenant or accountability group with colleagues or friends; serving as a spiritual friend, companion, or mentor to another person.

Gifts of the Mind

To love God with your mind is to search for greater understanding of God's wisdom and will for the world. Examples of spiritual practices might include: daily Bible study or devotional reading; spiritual reading of Scripture, such as *lectio divina*; scholarly research or writing on biblical, theological, historical, liturgical, or practical matters in the faith and life of the church.

To love your neighbor with your mind is to share with others in the pursuit of God's wisdom and truth. Examples of spiritual practices might include: teaching, whether through the educational ministries of the church or in an academic setting; tutoring at-risk students, giving music lessons, instruction in language-acquisition or life skills; taking part in a study group, game night, or book club in the congregation or local community.

Gifts of Strength

To love God with your strength is to embody prayer and praise in daily life. Examples of spiritual practices might include: physical exercise, walking, or dance as a form of prayer; disciplines of fasting, simplicity, and humility; care for God's creation through gardening, recycling, and the responsible and sustainable use of resources.

To love your neighbor with your strength is to devote one's energy and will to the well-being of others. Examples of spiritual practices might include: service projects, such as building or repairing a house, providing clean water, or improving sanitary conditions; volunteering in a soup kitchen, food pantry, or clothes closet; engaging in activism or public witness in order to effect positive changes in the community, nation, or world.

These examples are by no means intended to be conclusive, establishing rigid categories, or exhaustive, covering the whole range of spiritual experience. Who would dare to name or number the manifold gifts of the Spirit? My hope in presenting this array of examples is fourfold: first, to suggest a more expansive way of thinking about the varieties of gifts, services, and activities that comprise spiritual life in all its fullness and wholeness; second, to encourage individuals and congregations to be better stewards of the gifts of the Spirit in every aspect of Christian life and service; third, to help readers recognize ways in which they may *already* be living out the promise of their baptism; and fourth, to invite readers to consider "trying on" one or more of these practices as a new way of drawing nearer to God and neighbor.

One personal example: I'm a somewhat irregular reader of the daily lectionary provided in the Presbyterian *Book of Common Worship* and on the PC(USA) Daily Prayer app. I'm always glad and grateful for those seasons in my life when I make time for this spiritual discipline—and I've learned how to let go (another good spiritual discipline!) of the guilt I used to feel about not reading every day. (Perfectionism is the enemy of practice.) When I'm in the habit of reading, several remarkable things happen: key words from the appointed scriptures seem to pop up in casual conversation; prominent symbols and images change how I see the world; central themes affect how I interpret the events of the day; the voices of the biblical texts make their way into the voice of my own prayers; and every now and then, there is the wonderful revelation that a friend or colleague has been reading the same passages that day. As for those other times, when I'm not keeping up with the daily reading, I've come to trust that God is speaking to me in other ways. All of these are gifts from God, illumined by the same Spirit who attends and empowers our baptism.

The Gift of Worship

I saved the discussion of participation in public worship for last, not because it is least important, but because the church's worship is where it all comes together: hearts united in prayer and praise; souls joined in harmonious song; minds open to the teaching of the Word; strength given in service to the Spirit; neighbors assembled under one roof in the house of God, strangers welcomed and enemies reconciled by the grace of Christ; the sinful made holy and the broken made whole. We might think of participation in public worship as the foundation upon which all of the other practices and disciplines of faith are built, or the soil in which they are rooted and from which they grow to bear good fruit.

Worship itself is a gracious gift of God—the gift of being able to gather in God's presence, to hear again the gospel of Jesus Christ, to share in the communion of the Holy Spirit, and to be sent out to love and serve the Lord in daily life. God calls us to worship because God wants to be in relationship with us. God speaks to us through the Word so that we will know the truth that sets us free. God offers God's own self to us through the sacraments so that we might taste and see the goodness of the Lord. God sends us out to share the good news of Jesus with others through our words and deeds.

Worship is also the primary and central occasion in which we respond and lay claim to God's grace—singing thanksgiving and praise, confessing our sin and receiving Christ's mercy, crying out in supplication and lament, interceding for the church and world, calling on the transforming power of the Spirit. As emphasized above, we respond to God's grace, not as a dull obligation or chore, but with gratitude in the Spirit of love.

Worship is something like a school for prayer. In services of Christian worship, we practice our prayer, in order that we may learn to "pray without ceasing" (1 Thess. 5:17) in the service of daily living. The prayerful words and gestures of the liturgy form and reform our prayerful speech and action in the world. Indeed, almost anything can become a spiritual discipline when it is practiced prayerfully—as a way of opening our lives to the presence, power, and grace of God.

Worship might also be understood as a school for the stewardship of spiritual gifts: gathering in the church's sanctuary, we learn to be attentive to the presence of God in every place; confessing our sins and receiving the assurance of pardon, we learn to seek reconciliation in the world and forgive those who sin against us; hearing the Word read and proclaimed, we learn to recognize and listen for God's voice at all times; standing to affirm our faith, we learn to stand up and speak out for what is right; placing a financial contribution in the offering plate, we learn to place our lives in God's hands and offer ourselves in God's service; receiving the bread and cup at Christ's table, we learn to receive the grace of God as a gift and respond with great thanksgiving; going forth from the doors of the church, we learn to step out in faith and cross boundaries for the sake of the gospel; glorifying and enjoying God in worship, we learn the meaning and purpose of all life: to glorify and enjoy God forever.[8]

Ultimately, being a good steward of the gifts of the Spirit comes down to these six, simple words: "remember your baptism, and be thankful." Make good and faithful use of the spiritual gifts God has so freely poured out in your life. Draw near to the triune God of our baptism, and find yourself encircled by the communion of saints. Let your life be an outpouring of gratitude for the overflowing grace of Jesus Christ, a gift of love to the God from whom all blessings flow. Remember your baptism, and be thankful.

Questions for Reflection

1. Where is the Spirit already at work in your congregation or ministry context? What gifts have been poured out among, not just your leadership, but the entire community?
2. How are the gifts of your community celebrated and valued by the congregation? How are the gifts of youth and the elderly lifted up and celebrated?
3. In what ways does your congregation remember and celebrate baptism in your life together?

Applications for Life Together

- Leaders of confirmation or catechism classes may consider using the topic of baptism as an entry point for discussing spiritual gifts and the unique and beloved identity of each individual. Such discussions can extend to the entire congregation.

- Practice affirming the gifts you see in others. Affirmations may take shape as an organized activity in a group setting (either as written or spoken affirmations for each member of the group), in thank-you notes written to individuals who have shared their gifts with the community, or simply as part of regular conversation.

7

Stewardship of Body

On Flesh

ELLIE ROSCHER

My feet were still painfully swollen a week after my son was born. The skin stretched taut, it looked like someone else's feet were attached to my legs. While Simon napped, Dan, my spouse, brought a small tub of warm, soapy water over to the couch. He gently placed my feet in the tub. At his first touch, I crumbled in tears. I had endured two miscarriages and a hard pregnancy. I labored for fifty-eight hours before birthing a nine-and-a-half-pound baby via cesarean section. My body and spirit were tired. The emotion kept coming out of my body in waves. Surrendering to my fatigue, I wondered if I would ever reach the bottom of my grief.

Dan slowly, deliberately dabbed my feet dry, then massaged and rubbed lotion into each bulging foot. The gentle, affectionate attention felt like mercy. It reminded me that I had a body. After sharing my body for so long, it belonged to me again. I had to take stock of this new version of me, with new scars and memories, new milk and primal feelings of mother love surging through me. I thought of the woman who anointed Jesus' feet. How grateful he must have felt, in all his humanity, that someone finally touched him back with compassion and care and reminded him that he had a body, too.

Dan rose and kissed me twice. "Thank you," I whispered, still crying softly. He unlocked a clog that was holding my sorrow hostage. I was unstuck. The next morning he glanced down and said, "Look, your feet. They're back."

What does it mean to be stewards of our bodies? And what does it mean for our churches to equip and support communities in this journey inward? These questions are timely and venture us toward human-made walls that are holding us back. On our path to higher consciousness as individuals and societies, our disembodiment is limiting our potential.

Stewardship of the body plays out in daily micro-choices we make about how to treat our bodies. Food writer Michael Pollan calls us to body stewardship when he suggests we eat real food, mostly plants, and not too much.[1] People who can suspend the immediate gratification of processed foods high in syrup and salt, and opt to eat food that make their bodies feel good, tend to be healthier.

Digital media expert Erin Walsh calls us to body stewardship when she reminds people navigating the digital age that it's not about counting screen-time hours, it's about being able to unplug.[2] People who can turn off technology and enjoy spending time in their bodies tend to do better in the world.

Being stewards of our bodies is noticing how real food makes our bodies feel good. It has something to do with putting our phones down long enough to look each other in the face. It has something to do with being honest about where we are hanging out on the gradation scales of sugar and screen addictions. And maybe eating less meat and going out to play in the sun will inspire us to make other good decisions that are easier on all of God's creatures as well as the earth. There is a lot at stake when we choose whether to ignore or to embrace our bodies.

Claiming our bodies means intentionally embracing pleasure. Our bodies can identify six unique, vivid flavors in a single sip of complex red wine. They can take in the grandeur of a mountain range, causing an internal hushed sense of awe. Our shoulders relax at the first breath of spring, thawing our hearts and turning our chins back up to the heavens in hope. Our voices articulate thoughts from our minds. Our bodies experience pure ecstasy in lovemaking where we cease to be able to identify where one person ends and the other begins. Our ears process the intricate harmonies created by an orchestra, a sound powerful enough to transform our thoughts. Actively noticing the pleasure our bodies can cultivate changes our mind-set—and dare I say worldview—harboring a gratitude for the body and a sense of abundance in the world.

Stewardship means appreciating the brilliance of bodies. Bodies are smart, often smarter than we give them credit for. Consider athletes and actors who work to suspend thought in order to clear up room for purer, unencumbered physical genius. Consider the communication that happens between a baby's body and a mother's body during pregnancy and breast-feeding. Or the body's ability to warn us of danger, maintain homeostasis, stay alive with numerous involuntary and continuous actions. Bodies are nothing short of astounding.

We comprehend and apply meaning to the world because of our bodies, our senses. We know that we are individuals dwelling among others. With skin as a boundary, our bodies are homes to experiences, memories, and beliefs. We experience the world as part of the world, as in the world. It is our bodies that exist in the world and inform the inner self.

Our bodies are not a hindrance to knowledge, but the vehicles with which the self exists and acquires knowledge. I can approach my body with reverence, curiosity, honesty, and awe. I can see my body clearly as an instrument of knowledge. Taking the posture of reverence and wonder is what I consider stewardship of the body.

The Wisdom of Bodies

I have been actively aware of my body as a gift for as long as I can remember. After watching Mary Lou Retton win the 1984 Olympic gold medal, my parents put me—an enraptured four-year-old—in gymnastics. I instantly fell in love, and was competing by age seven. I loved flipping and flying and twisting. I loved sweating and leaping and watching my muscles emerge. I remember coming down off the trampo-line, thinking, "I can't believe most people go through life without ever knowing what flying feels like."

Then, at age thirteen, I fell. I over-rotated on a new tumbling pass, put my arm out to brace my fall, and watched it fly out of joint at the elbow. I passed out, and woke to paramedics checking my cognition. I couldn't feel my left hand. After a painful ambulance ride to the hospital, I remember a chaotic emergency room with a lot of poking and prodding. I remember shots to the armpit to numb my arm. I remember waking to dull pain and a horribly bright orange cast.

Physical therapy was horrendous. Three days a week my therapist used deep tissue massage, heat, his aggressively applied pressure, and heavy weights to get my joint to straighten out. The trauma to the elbow caused tightness that wouldn't give, and the joint started calcifying. I sat in the doctor's office in my plaid, Catholic grade-school uniform expressing my frustration.

"Why won't my arm straighten? I need to get back into the gym."

The doctor took a deep breath, and told me my elbow was healing too well, too quickly. My body was producing more calcification of bone than the joint could flush back out. He told me that the injury was more complicated than the combination double dislocation and compound fracture. The night of the injury, the joint had cut off circulation to my hand for so long that the tissue was dying. They were planning to amputate my arm just above the elbow. In a last-ditch effort to save my arm, the doctor jostled the joint around forcefully. It worked. I got a pulse back in my wrist, and they didn't have to amputate.

In a single moment, I went from feeling sorry for myself because of my limitation to feeling overwhelmingly grateful for the gift of my arms. I went on to have a successful college gymnastics career despite my slightly bent left arm. And ever since, I have walked through life marveling that I have two arms, marveling at what my body can do.

My body is human. It's broken and limited. It's imperfect, but it's mine. God is God, and I am not, but I am strong. My body breaks, but it heals too. Inside my body, I have experienced new life.

When my gymnastics career ended, I started running marathons. After months of training, I finally crossed the first finish line, filled with a pride that whispered, "No one will ever be able to take this feat away from you." Pushing the limits of the body God gave me was the first lesson. Learning how to rest that body was the second. Marathon running turned to yoga. Like gymnastics and running, yoga also quieted my mind and fed my soul. It was a time set apart when my mind-soul-body coexisted and cultivated strength, peace, and calm inside. Yoga was a real spiritual practice in which I was elevated to a place where my body informed my being.

My yoga instructor taught me to approach my arm, bent for decades, with humility. "Your elbow is now your guru," he said. "Your job is to listen to it. In striving for health, it will teach you about yourself, about compassion and perseverance." It was refreshing that he undauntedly approached my misfit body with attention and knowledge, ready to teach and challenge. It diffused the silent power of my limitations and made combatting them playful and productive. His attention to my body invited me to pay attention too.

My body speaks loudly to get my attention. Styes, migraines, canker sores, and shingles tell me it's well past time to slow down. Fifteen years after my elbow injury, I crushed my hand in a piece of gymnastics equipment. Months into healing, the doctor looked at a mound of scar tissue on my palm and repeated what the doctor had said about my elbow, "You healed too quickly."

Healing can't be rushed. Neither can love or art or justice. My mind is wired to prioritize speed and efficiency above all. My body brings me back to the truth, repeatedly whispering over and over again, *slow down*. I rub the little bump on my palm whenever I grow impatient with my journey. It is a worthy endeavor to tend to my body and listen to it and trust that the lessons it has for me will bring me to a better version of myself.

Bodies Matter to God

Bodies are a gift from God. How we talk to our bodies, treat them, and care for them is how we respond to that gift. It's a form of prayer. Our bodies are powerful if we pay attention to them. I take my body seriously. God takes my body seriously too.

Bodies matter to God. In our creation stories, we see that the creation of our bodies took time and contemplation, mud and breath. God knit us together in our mothers' wombs, one cell at a time. God knows every hair on our heads. God creates our bodies in God's image and looks at us and says we are indeed *very* good. God worked with Adam over time and with effort to create a suitable body to be his partner. There is tenderness in God's knowledge of our bodies.

Against all human comprehension, God chose to take on a body, become flesh, and walk around with us as a human being—a real human being with a real human body. It was a bold move, unexpected, a game changer. This radical act of love, coming to us as a vulnerable, dependent, mortal baby is so audacious, in fact, that the humanity of Jesus is one thing we have been arguing about for centuries. We can't quite believe it. Our God knows our bodies because God had a body. And now nothing—not even the death of our bodies—can separate us from the love of God.

I was sitting still among quiet, stoic Norwegian Lutherans one Sunday during worship. My ears perked up as Pastor Kris started talking about what we so rarely talk about in church: bodies.

> Yesterday, I fished a tampon out of a toilet. It was one of those days, one of those weeks. We had the funeral for a fifteen-year-old boy who died on Monday. Eight hundred people showed up. Hundreds of teenagers, hundreds of parents, multitudes from the

community came to support the family and to weep. Numb and uncertain, it was a swirl of sorrow. When almost everyone had gone home, I happened upon this remnant from the day—a blood-stained, water-logged feminine product that was deposited where we all know it's not supposed to go. But who could blame this fragile, young woman trying to make sense of the unfathomable? And why should the custodian be left to deal with everyone's refuse? There is dignity in caring for one another's needs—even body needs. We wipe one another's tears, and we hold each other. So I went to the nursery and found some latex gloves, then rescued this artifact of our embodied lives. We're freed to love and serve each other; that's what the Gospel tells us. It was something tangible on a grief-stricken day, so I said yes—to community, to these kids, and to our life together. Even if it's messy, we'll figure it out as we go along.[3]

My church addresses bodies by having a parish nurse on staff, and offering programs like gentle yoga. These are steps. But hearing my pastor say the word *tampon* from the pulpit was so utterly refreshing that I know we still have work to do.

There's a lot at stake. Our minds and souls have something to benefit from our bodies being taken seriously. There is a real, deep, pervasive fear of bodies in our society and our church. The undercurrent tells us to ignore our bodies and not spend time talking about or tending to them. The consequences of not identifying and uprooting this fear are grim. Body estrangement plays a role in obesity and eating disorders and unhealthy sexual behaviors and addictions. In order to address racism, misogyny, and homophobia, we must acknowledge our bodies.

It quickly gets overwhelming. We try to keep ignoring the problem, in part because the uprooting is tiring, time-consuming work. To become stewards of our bodies, we have to travel back in our Christian ancestry to understand the source. It helps to identify and understand factors hindering us from the awe and appreciation of our bodies that steward-ship requires.[4]

We need look only to Song of Solomon to get a sense of how bodies were celebrated in pre-Christian Hebrew life. The Greeks, however, embraced a mind-body dualism that we are still working to identify and eradicate. Plato introduced a dis-tinction between the sacredness of love that comes from the soul and the profanity of love that comes from the body. The mind is pure, while the body is dirty. Stoics promoted pas-sionless lives. They were skeptical of excitement. Sex was sup-posed to strictly be about procreation. These threads deeply affected the forming of the Christian Church.

When taken out of historical context, it's easy to read Paul's contrasting of the spirit and the flesh as supporting dualism—the spirit is pure and the flesh is impure. Yet in Paul's the-ology, the body is central. For Paul, salvation, forgiveness, renewal, and resurrection are all things that happen to and through bodies.

Leaders in the early church, unlike Paul, tended to be very harsh on bodies. They thought the end times were near, and this small church differentiated itself from the rest of society. Virginity, chastity, purity, piety, and ultimately martyrdom were all virtues of the early church. Our sexuality was tied to The Fall, so God resided in our good souls and not in our fallen bodies. Augustine, in particular, focused on lust and tied sex to original sin. He was suspicious of how pleasure was able to override reason, and quarantined sex to procreation.

We see dualism throughout the Middle Ages in specific physical penance for particular sins, punishing the body for its temporary invasion over the mind's logic and reason. And although marriage was named a sacrament, Aquinas makes clear that sex within a marriage should be solely for procre-ation. Luther, wary of his own libido, also connected sex to lust and the fallen human. Calvin, although acknowledging the unity-building aspect of sex, still restricted the physical enjoyment to the context of a proper marriage. Meanwhile, the Catholic Church categorized sex for procreation as "in accordance to nature." Sexual sins like fornication, rape, and incest were lesser sins than masturbation, bestiality, and homosexual sex because the former could lead to procreation and the latter—sins contrary to nature—could not. Dualism continued to reign. The mind and the body were separate. The mind was holy, bringing us closer to God. The body was sinful, tugging us toward hell.

The church didn't stay small, and the end times did not come. Yet the idea that man is superior to woman and mind is superior to body pervaded the growing church so deeply that we are still rooted in disembodiment today. The two ideas became intertwined. Women were associated with the body. Men were associated with the mind. The worst thing a man could be was feminine, dwelling in the body. We have let ourselves get away from our Hebrew roots, which were not skeptical of bodies. Dualism is alive and well today in our churches. Implications of dualism range from physical deprivation of all kinds as religious practice, to seemingly God-ordained, Bible-backed misogyny and homophobia, to standing still in worship. We take Communion, the body of Christ, without letting that nourishment transform how we talk to, or treat, or act in, our own bodies.

The history of disembodiment in the church is supported and grounded in a society out of touch with our bodies. The man sitting still at his desk is often valued higher and paid more than the man working with his hands. Childhood obesity is on the rise, as are obesity-related illnesses in adults. We eat our food on the go without tasting it, we buy gym memberships without changing our habits, we ignore headaches by popping more Advil, and we fall into the couch to relax to hours of television every night. I have to imagine God's vision for our lives incorporates our bodies. Won't body wellness contribute to us becoming our best, most authentic selves?

I studied the work of Augustine, Paul, and Calvin. I've read the *Catechism of the Catholic Church*. Dualism never took hold in me because it was absolutely foreign to my experience of my mind and body being deeply connected in ways that indeed brought me closer to God. Fighting dualism is a complex, layered battle that requires attention at the individual and communal level. At the core of our disembodiment, there is also a people privileged enough to take our bodies for granted. Here, Pierre Bourdieu's articulation of *habitus* is quite helpful.[5]

Our bodies are socialized, constantly responding to external stimuli, playing roles in our different habitats. Our bodies mimic others like us, and are capable of learning to act collectively, in a highly detailed and orchestrated way.

Habitus, an inner memory pad of sorts, is a way of being in relationship with the world. The social world inscribes itself on the habitus, which responds to and is created by our social environment. Bourdieu believes the habitus, the embodiment of social influences, has inertia and can be perpetuated throughout history. Those whose habitus is aligned with their environment can experience happiness. When in the company of like-minded people, for example, we trust our bodies and can take them for granted. When we find ourselves in a new situation or environment, we become more conscious of our posturing and think about the appropriateness of its movements.

I was born into the world with societal power. I am a white, heterosexual, cisgender, able-bodied, wealthy Christian with two attractive parents who love me. There is a bodily ease that comes with being "well born." I can trust my disposition and not waste energy wondering how to play the game I have found myself in. I don't have to recognize my body, and that is the clearest mark of privilege. My social world allowed my habitus to come into its own.

I did not have the vernacular yet, but I thought a great deal about my habitus while working at a day shelter for women in Denver. One day, for example, I went to work without my nametag. As women entered the room, they would walk right up to me and talk to me as if they knew I was staff. I finally asked one woman how she knew I worked there. "I can just tell," she said. "Life has been easy for you."

She was right. I had never been homeless or hungry. I had never worried about my survival. I had the posture of an aristocrat. The game of life was working for me, so I could take my body for granted. The loop between my habitus and my habitat reinforced my ease in life. I mattered. I was smart and good. I had power. My world confirmed those inner beliefs. My body took on that shape. The clients, on the other hand, had to keep watch, consciously thinking about their behavior as they navigated a social-service agency run by people of power. That vigilance is tiring, adding fatigue to an already grueling life of poverty.

Much of the Christian church in the United States enjoys privilege. Unlike our Jewish and Muslim brothers and sisters, whom Bourdieu would say have "marked" habitus, my habitus as a Christian is unmarked in the United States. It is durable, calm and quiet. Without conscious effort, I can easily become disembodied because I have the privilege to choose whether or not to notice it.

We can get back to the sense that our bodies are a gift from God. Claiming and loving our bodies as beautiful and powerful responds to that gift from God. Our bodies are ours to enjoy, ours with which to serve. We in the church today have an opportunity to be the leaders, the spokespeople for truth and healing. In order to do so, we have to acknowledge our history of dualism and privilege. We have to talk about the color of our skin and our sexuality. We can deny dualism because we don't worship Augustine or Luther. We worship Jesus as Messiah. And bodies matter to Jesus.

Bodies Matter to Jesus

We see Jesus' attention to bodies in his healing ministry. By bringing sight to the blind and hearing to the deaf, by curing leprosy and paralysis, straightening withered hands and calling unclean spirits out of people, by stopping the flow of blood and bringing people back to life, he restored not only their health but also their status in society. He recognized women and children, immigrants and the disabled. He brought people on the margins back into the center of society. He used his own spit to heal. Power seeped from him readily, flowing even from his cloak. And so often he chose to heal tenderly, with a gentle human touch that many must have so deeply craved in a society that shunned and blamed them for their afflictions.

Bodies matter in Jesus' life and also in his death. He was disrobed and whipped and spat on and ridiculed and ultimately put to death like a common criminal. Jesus cried out to God, feeling forsaken. That sense of abandonment was real and felt, in his being, in his body. God looked at Jesus' body on the cross, in the shape of a slave, and called Jesus "Lord." In the Christ Hymn, we get a glimpse of what the early church proclaimed as true:

> Let the same mind be in you that was in Christ Jesus,
>   who, though he was in the form of God,
>   did not regard equality with God
>   as something to be exploited,
>   but emptied himself
>   taking the form of a slave,
>   being born in human likeness.
> And being found in human form,
>   he humbled himself
>   and became obedient to the point of death—
>   even death on a cross. (Phil. 2:5–8)

We're talking about bodies. Jesus took the posture of a slave, empting his body of his divinity so that we might know our God as fully human. By lowering himself from God to slave, Jesus erased all human-made boundaries. There had to be a real, tangible—not "as if"—crucifixion. Jesus couldn't just go through the motions, if he wanted to offer us eternal life. He couldn't just hand it over and say, "Here, take my divinity. Have eternal life." We never would have understood that. Taking on the darkness of humanity, experiencing death as a slave and enduring it, he handed divinity over to us, the very ones who deserve it the least.

And then, later, there was this lovely moment when Jesus allowed Thomas to touch his wounds. I'm grateful for Thomas's desire for evidence. It's such a human reaction, so that we too can witness Jesus' resurrected body. His body, with wounds still fresh, rose from the dead. His resurrected body radiates with good news.

Bodies play a pivotal role in Jesus' life, death, and resurrection. We believe that Jesus, fully God and fully human, suffered and died and rose again. At the center of our faith is suffering, so that at the center of our faith can be love. Jesus took on a body so that we could fall in love with him. In Communion we are reminded of this gift, sustained by Jesus' body and blood.

As followers of Jesus, as worshipers of God, as students of the Song of Solomon, we the church can lead the way back to our bodies. The courageous journey can bring healing and reconciliation, abounding with wonder and awe.

When my son was a few months old, I would bring him into bed with me each morning and watch him wake up. I loved the stretch of time when he was discovering his hands. He held his hands right in front of his unblinking eyes, rotating them slowly to study each finger in a way that invited me into the revelry.

"I know, Simon, I know," I'd coo. "Aren't your hands amazing? Aren't we just so lucky to have hands? So cool, Simon. So cool. You are going to do amazing things with those hands in your life. You have feet, too! And a whole body, and another day in that body to play, play, play. Isn't it grand?"

My eyes filled with tears.

I believe it for him. I believe it for me.

Questions for Reflection

1. In what ways are human bodies engaged in the life of the community of your congregation? How does your community promote health and wholeness of bodies?
2. How does your congregation talk about sexuality? In what ways might you consider further conversation? How would you frame it with an awareness of the stewardship of our bodies?

3. What does it mean to be stewards of our bodies? How might the church equip disciples to care for and attend to bodies?

Applications for Life Together

- Launch an education series on topics such as: bodies in the Hebrew Scriptures, human sexuality and Christianity, Pauline understanding of the body, body and sacraments, embodied spiritual practices.
- Experiment with ways to name and claim the embodied nature of worship. Options might include drawing attention to the embodied nature of singing, kneeling, and praying; using incense or fresh-baked Communion bread; anointing with oil; laying on of hands; movement or dance.

8

Stewardship of Community

Investing Social Capital as an Act of Faith

JOHN W. VEST

As mainline, evangelical, and Catholic forms of Christianity continue to decline relative to the overall population of the United States, giving rise to increasingly high numbers of people who claim no religious affiliation—often referred to as "nones"—a question emerges. Why, if at all, does church matter? When I pose this question to people who still participate in church on a regular basis, by far the most common answer I receive has something to do with community. To be sure, churchgoers also value worship, the sacraments, religious education, spiritual formation, inspiration, moral guidance, and opportunities for service. But when pushed to consider what they would miss the most about church were it to no longer exist as we now know it, the majority of Christians I encounter invoke the relationships and mutual support they experience in their communities of faith.

Anthropologists, sociologists, psychologists, and neuroscientists have developed numerous ways of amplifying Aristotle's ancient insight that human beings are fundamentally social animals. Centuries before Aristotle, a Hebrew theologian and poet proposed that human beings were created in

106

the image of a mysteriously plural deity—or at the very least, a God in intimate communion with other divine or celestial beings (Gen. 1:26–27). Centuries later, Christian theologians suggested that human beings and human relationships are iconic reflections of the relational nature of a triune God—one God in three persons. Today quantum physicists are discovering that relationships of energy, which often behave in unexpected and (thus far) unexplainable ways, are the true building blocks of the universe.[1] Relationships, it seems, are foundational for all of creation. We are relational beings living in a relational world.

From quantum entanglement to your circle of closest associations to the global village of which we are all a part, community is a precious gift of God. Indeed, community may be the key that helps us pierce the veil and peer into the deepest mysteries of the divine. What we do with this gift is an act of faith. How we relate with others says something about our relationship with God. Nurturing community is therefore a vital element of the holistic understanding of stewardship explored in this book.

From the early years of colonial America and persisting for more than three centuries as a key ingredient in the social infrastructure of the United States, churches and other religious institutions have been centers and shapers of community life. To this day, many congregations operate as if creating and cultivating community is one of their primary tasks. However, while religious leaders acknowledge that the church now exists in a very different cultural situation, few recognize that there is a fundamental disconnect between the changing nature of community in today's world and our inherited forms of congregational life. Because an increasing number of people no longer turn to religious congregations as a primary locus of community, I will argue that churches no longer need to focus on *creating* community. Rather, God is calling us—*as stewards of community*—to participate in *existing* communities as the body of Christ in the world.

Different Understandings of Church and Community

A couple of years ago, my friend Greg Bolt invited me to preach at the church he pastored in Nebraska City, Nebraska. I was serving a congregation in downtown Chicago in those days, so visiting this small midwestern town felt to me like going back in time.

The home of Arbor Day, Nebraska City is the oldest incorporated city in the state and has a population of just over 7,200. It maintains the kind of small-town layout once common in the United States. Taking up a full block in the exact center of town is the Otoe County Courthouse, a picturesque two-story red brick building surrounded by grass lawns and full trees. It is, quite literally, the public square of Nebraska City. Across the street from the courthouse is the church Greg pastors, First Presbyterian. Founded in 1855, this congregation is as old as the town and boasts the first church bell in Nebraska. A block east of the church is the public library and middle school. Family businesses, convenience stores, local restaurants, fast food chains, a movie theater, and several banks can all be found within a few blocks. Just as close—walking distance, in fact—are several other churches: Faith Baptist Church, St. Mary's Episcopal Church, First United Methodist Church, First Christian Church, First Baptist Church, First Evangelical Lutheran Church, St. Mary's Catholic Church, and the Nebraska City Seventh-day Adventist Church. Nebraska City is a reminder of what some people still think of as the good old days of American Christendom.

Compare this to Faith Chapel Christian Center (FCCC) in Birmingham, Alabama, a nondenominational megachurch with a membership approaching the total population of Nebraska City. FCCC began in 1981 in the home of its pastor, Michael Moore. In 1999, the congregation purchased 37.6 acres of land in Birmingham's Wylam neighborhood, and in 2002, they completed their 3,000-seat "Word Dome" sanctuary, the largest diameter monolithic dome in the world. In 2003, they purchased an additional one hundred acres for "The Bridge," a sixteen-acre "family life complex" consisting of six additional domes. Completed in 2011 and opened to the public in 2014, this multipurpose space includes a twelve-lane bowling alley, a café, an NBA-sized basketball court, a fitness center with an indoor track, the largest climbing wall in North America, an indoor playground for children, a banquet facility, a teen dance club, and a smoke- and alcohol-free nightclub for adults.

These two congregations represent very different understandings of the relationship between church and community. First Presbyterian's location at the center of town is indicative of the role it played—and in some ways continues to play—in Nebraska City. It was a cornerstone institution at the physical and social center of community life, surrounded by similar anchor institutions. It was likely a place of intersection and civic engagement. Automobiles didn't arrive in Nebraska City until after 1900, so for fifty years townspeople would have passed each other on foot or by horse on their way to church and other public spaces. These days, most people drive from place to place, and First Presbyterian Church has become one of several options community members can choose from for religious devotion and community service. While its shrinking and aging membership and average worship attendance reflect the rise and subsequent decline of mainline Protestant churches in the United States in the century and a half since its founding, First Presbyterian still bears many marks of the kind of community church that was an integral element in the social infrastructure on which the United States was built.

Only thirty-five years old—with even less time in its current campus—Faith Chapel Christian Center is relatively new on the Birmingham scene. Located in a depressed and low-income neighborhood, FCCC is less of a cornerstone institution and more of a self-contained alternative to or refuge from the surrounding community. Indeed, its purposefully named recreation and entertainment complex—The Bridge—is intended to fill a social void in the neighborhood. "We believe we can really meet the needs of the community," notes their pastor. "It will bridge people from the world to the kingdom. People may not want to come to a church, but they'll come to a bowling alley. People have needs other than spiritual needs. There's a need for safe, clean, uplifting, family-oriented entertainment."[2] FCCC is like a Christian colony in the midst of a foreign land. While the church certainly engages in a variety of community service endeavors like hunger and homelessness ministries, the theological underpinning of The Bridge has more to do with separatism or escapism than with cultural transformation.

Every congregation can be analyzed in this way to reveal how it relates—intentionally or unintentionally—to its surrounding community. The same is true of the way we prioritize relationships in our personal lives. As with all of the resources explored in this book, congregations and individual Christians have choices to make when it comes to community. How we understand community, where and with whom we spend our time, and which types of relationships we invest in are all questions with significant theological implications. A helpful way to understand these choices is the notion of "social capital."

The Redistribution of Social Capital

Although it has been used by cultural observers and sociologists for more than a century, the concept of social capital is best known through the work of Robert Putnam and his influential book *Bowling Alone: The Collapse and Revival of American Community*.[3] "Whereas physical capital refers to physical objects and human capital refers to properties of individuals," wrote Putnam, "social capital refers to connections among individuals—social networks and the norms of reciprocity and trustworthiness that arise from them."[4] As described by Putnam, social capital is best understood as the aggregate value, strength, and power of interpersonal relationships in North American society.

Through numerous examples and studies, Putnam argues that Americans have become increasingly disconnected from one another and, therefore, more isolated and estranged. Unprecedented pressures regarding time and money,

suburban sprawl, and longer commutes, personalized entertainment, and generational change have all contributed to the
erosion of civic engagement and informal social connections,
thereby reducing the nation's reserves of social capital. Putnam is especially attuned to the decline of social, civic, and
religious membership-based organizations. Because social
capital has both personal and public benefits, its depletion
is harmful for both individuals and for society as a whole.
Human flourishing, civil discourse, and democracy are all
dependent upon social capital. Its loss, Putnam suggests, is a
dangerous trend that must be reversed.

Formulated before the explosion of digital, social-media
platforms and increasingly mobile computing and communications technologies, Putnam's conclusions are not the only
way to understand the significant social changes we have experienced in recent decades. Instead of community in decline, it
is more likely that we are simply witnessing community being
redefined. In particular, group-based relationships are being
replaced by porous institutions and the loose connections of
social networks.[5] In fact, Lee Rainie and Barry Wellman have
recently proposed that "networked individualism" is the "new
social operating system" of the twenty-first century. "The
hallmark of networked individualism is that people function
more as connected individuals and less as embedded group
members."[6] This doesn't mean that people are necessarily
isolated or hyper-individualistic. Rather, it means that instead
of connecting with others primarily through groups—including neighborhood, work, civic, and religious groups—people
develop numerous, multilayered, fragmented, and constantly
shifting personal social networks of less intimate connections.

Marc Dunkelman has taken this line of thinking even further.[7] Building on the "social brain hypothesis" of anthropolo-
gist Robin Dunbar—who makes it clear that social networks
have existed from the beginning of human civilization and
should not be primarily associated with digital, social-media
platforms—Dunkelman uses the rings of Saturn as a metaphor for the three primary types of relationships that shape
our social lives. "Inner-ring" relationships are our relatively

few and most intimate connections: family, best friends, and our closest colleagues and coworkers. "Middle-ring" relationships are familiar but not intimate—the kinds of affiliations that comprised traditional villages and the "township" social architecture that Alexis de Tocqueville concluded was a key innovation in the development of American society. Finally, "outer-ring" relationships are the more numerous acquaintances and weak ties that populate the rest of our social networks. These are often based on shared interests or activities. Dunkelman suggests that the crisis Putnam described is actually the deprioritization of middle-ring relationships—which most people equate with traditional notions of "community"—but not an abandonment of all forms of social interaction. In place of these middle-ring affiliations, Americans are devoting more attention to inner- and outer-ring connections.

To explain this phenomenon, Dunkelman offers a slightly different take on the concept of social capital: "Rather than imagine it as a gross measure of a society's connective tissue, we should think of it as we think of, well, capital. Social capital should be defined quite simply as the amount of time and attention an individual devotes to a range of human interaction. We should think of it as something that, like money, we control and invest."[8] Because humans have a biologically and psychologically limited supply of social capital, we cannot possibly invest equally in all of the relationships that make up our social networks. Some will necessarily be prioritized at the expense of others.

Beginning with the Industrial Revolution and the advent of the automobile, traditional forms of group-based community—which go all the way back to the development of agriculture—have been on the decline. Telephones, radio, and television, inexpensive air travel, the Internet, and mobile technologies have only accelerated this phenomenon as it becomes easier and easier to invest in relationships of choice rather than relationships of proximity. While these developments allow us to avoid the inefficiencies and hassles of village and township entanglements, Dunkelman argues that it was precisely these inefficient middle-ring relationships that helped Americans work together for the common good for three and a half centuries.

With the cultural revolutions of the 1960s and subsequent shifts away from group-based communities in favor of networked individualism, things began to change. The loss of civility in public discourse, unprecedented levels of ideological polarization, and our gridlocked political system are some of the many examples of how this redistribution of social capital has affected the United States. These changes have created an unsettling sense of destabilization, amplified by the fact that the core institutions that long held together American society—religious institutions among them—are all based on middle-ring relationships, rendering them out of sync with the way more and more people choose to invest their social capital today.

Not only does this social capital analysis help us understand the massive cultural shifts that have reshaped American society in the past half-century, Dunkelman's insights also provide a framework to guide our faithful stewardship of community. If time and our capacity for meaningful relationships are finite resources—and, most important, precious gifts from God—then we must be wise in how we spend them. And if it is true that the erosion of middle-ring relationships and institutions are diminishing our capacity to work together for the common good—a key ingredient in the transformation of the world Jesus described as the emergence of God's kingdom—then we have at least two options before us: reprioritize middle-ring forms of community, or reimagine and relocate "church" to exist within the stronger inner- and outer-ring networks that are reshaping the nature of community in today's world.

Reinvesting in Middle-Ring Relationships

Examples of middle-ring reinvestment already exist in a variety of forms. The most radical approach is exemplified by the new monastic movement. In these intentional Christian communities, people live together in a common space or in close proximity and share many or all of their material resources. They enjoy regular communal meals and commit themselves to shared spiritual disciplines. While some critics suggest that these communities are as escapist as the Christian communes of the 1960s and 1970s, members of new monastic communities counter that they are dedicated to missional engagement in local neighborhoods. Proximity and stability—both of which are notably absent from the social networks of most Americans—are hallmarks of this movement. New monastics do not expect all Christians to follow this path, but they hope to model for the wider church—and world—how to reclaim traditional elements of community that have been lost.[9]

Less radical than new monasticism is the missional shift toward prioritizing the neighborhoods in which churches are located.[10] This can take the form of creative new worshiping communities[11] or through new understandings of mission in existing congregations. Recent decades have seen the rise of "missional communities" in which small groups of people gather for worship and very localized community engagement.[12] Sometimes these missional communities exist as subunits of a larger congregation or network, and sometimes they exist independently.[13]

Other approaches are even more common. For many years, medium- and large-sized congregations have used small groups to foster a better sense of community among members. In fact, this has been a very intentional community-building strategy among megachurches. In addition to small-group ministries, churches with above-average memberships often add one or more worship services as another way to make a congregation feel more intimate. Some churches encourage members to reclaim middle-ring relationships by practicing the "art of neighboring."[14] Others advocate for localized expressions of "slow church," based on the "slow food"—locavore—movement.[15]

Faith-based community organizing is yet another way churches can build and invest social capital. After years of cultural disestablishment and even marginalization, individual congregations may not possess the same level of social influence they did in the past. Yet community organizing continues to demonstrate that multiple religious groups working together can identify and address a variety of community challenges.[16]

A Fundamental Mismatch

Unless the trajectory of American society somehow makes a radical shift away from networked individualism, efforts to build or rebuild middle-ring relationships in neighborhoods and faith communities will be at odds with prevailing cultural norms and social practices. While it is true that the gospel has always been countercultural, Christians have also made good use of the cultures in which we find ourselves. One could say that Christians have been good stewards of culture.

The relatively modest movement initiated by Jesus "went viral" because it was—and is—highly adaptable for a variety of contexts and situations. Paul and the early missionaries took advantage of the infrastructure of the Roman Empire to spread the good news from community to community, creating a network of churches that were both deeply connected and uniquely local. In ways we are often not so proud of today, the collusion of church and empire we call Christendom extended this network to a global scale. In the United States, the township model of middle-ring relationships, which de Tocqueville identified as essential to the revolutionary rise and proliferation of New World democracy, both utilized and expanded the social capital of congregations and religious institutions. This form of American Christendom reached its zenith in the post–World War II baby boom, when part of what it meant to be a good citizen was to be a member of a local church.

Yet in numerous ways this cultural establishment of Christianity has been unraveling in the United States—a phenomenon we call post-Christendom—for the past half century. One of the clearest ways to observe this is the institutional decline of organized religion. While there are a number of reasons for this decline—both internal and external to the church—few church leaders realize that a significant contributing factor is a fundamental mismatch between the social architecture of traditional congregations and the new social operating system of networked individualism.

Polls and studies continue to report that Americans remain overwhelmingly faithful, measured in terms of belief in a higher power and spiritual practices like prayer and meditation. People are not giving up on God, but many have lost interest in church. Most faith leaders seem to think this has to do with content, which gives rise to church growth strategies based on more appealing or relevant worship services and programs. Because of this, mainline Protestants, denominational evangelicals, nondenominational megachurches, and even expressions of the more culturally attuned, emerging church movement all continue to invest social capital in a form of community that no longer reflects how an increasing number of people connect and interact with one another. There are limited returns on this investment because churches are essentially all competing with one another for a shrinking portion of the population—namely, people who are still interested in this increasingly anachronistic form of community.

I recently served on the advisory board for a local campus ministry. Month after month the minister would lament the fact that only a handful of students were coming to the Bible studies and worship services held each week—even when the ministry provided free food, the traditional church-bait for youth and young adults. Such frustrations echo those of many congregations and ministries that continue to organize programs that once attracted crowds but no longer seem to generate much interest. After hearing the campus minister's report, we came upon a new possibility. We asked him how many students he knew on campus, not just those who came to his programs. "About thirty-five," he responded. "Great! That's your congregation," we said. "What if, instead of investing a significant amount of time and energy in programs few students embraced, we work to find other ways of being in relationship with them in their own social contexts?" This paradigm shift challenges the church—and its leaders—to a new way of being.

We live in a culture in which more and more people prioritize inner- and outer-ring relationships, yet most of our churches are designed as middle-ring communities. In fact, this disconnect is true for many of the institutions that have shaped American culture, which results in the profound sense of destabilization—even crisis—social commentators regularly invoke. As Dunkelman notes, "[I]t feels as though things are falling apart because institutions built for township society don't work without the middle rings."[17] The question, then, is how to reshape these institutions to leverage our stronger inner- and outer-ring relationships. This is the adaptive challenge of being church in today's world.

Framing this as a question of stewardship reveals an important insight. If stewardship is about faithfully and responsibly deploying resources that God has created and gifted to us, the church must realize that it often no longer needs to *create* community and can instead focus on living missionally in communities *that already exist*. In today's world, these communities tend to be found in our inner- and outer-ring sets of relationships.

Except for extreme cases of social isolation, every human being exists in some form of community. For centuries, the church played a critical role in building and sustaining local communities. But long gone are the days in which towns like Nebraska City relied on cornerstone institutions like First Presbyterian Church to function as a center and shaper of community and culture. And most churches have neither the resources nor the need to create buildings and programs that compete with or replace entertainment and other social gathering spaces like we see at Faith Chapel Christian Center. When it comes to community, the forces that once formed these congregations have shifted. They risk seeming out of place in today's world.

People may no longer join civic or religious organizations in our culture of networked individuals, but they still value and nurture community in a variety of inner- and outer-ring relationships. If people are less inclined to "come to church," followers of Jesus must learn how to "be church" among the people.

Post-Christendom Missionaries

A good example of being church in existing outer-ring communities is Team Sweaty Sheep. Created in Louisville, Kentucky, and now expanding to Santa Cruz, California, Sweaty Sheep began as a ministry among athletes who experience God in running and other endurance events. Though they sometimes interact with traditional congregations and engage in familiar Christian practices, most of their faith formation happens while pursuing active lifestyles.

> Be it through worship, travel, laughter, prayer, running, dancing, or the like we seek to enjoy life by embracing the "abundance" Jesus yearned for us to know. From interactive worship services (indoors and outdoors) to Bible studies, from pre-race prayers to post-race parties, from mission trips to gardening, from quiet prayer and yoga to loud concerts and marathons—we seek to experience the divine in new, exciting, and unique ways![18]

Based on a philosophy they call "re-creation through recreation," they focus on activities that typically generate outer-ring relationships. By investing social capital in these relationships, pastor Ryan Althaus and Sweaty Sheep have transformed existing communities into faith communities that creatively connect with people who might not otherwise participate in a traditional congregation-based church. As they put it, "A church isn't a building, but a group of people who have been called by God for a purpose."[19]

The possibilities of this kind of community-based ministry were made clear to me several years ago when I experimented with an unconventional outreach event. For nine years I served a congregation in downtown Chicago, and for most of those years I drove past Soldier Field on my way to church on Sunday. When the Bears were playing at home, I could smell the pre-game tailgating festivities from several miles down the road on Lake Shore Drive. As a football fan and BBQ enthusiast, I confess that on many of those Sunday mornings I drove past the stadium longing to be there more than at church.

One Sunday, the Bears were playing a rare mid-afternoon game that I ended up attending with several of my pastor friends. As we stood around a table on the parking deck—eating, drinking, and preparing to engage in a variety of secular rituals—it occurred to me that even though the content was very different, our gathering bore some formal similarities to what we were doing just a few hours earlier—standing around a table of food and drink, engaging in a variety of sacred rituals. Based on my theological conviction that God is not confined to buildings made by human hands and is therefore just as present at a football stadium as at a church, I proposed an outreach event during which we would offer a worship service with Communion in the midst of tailgating before a Bears game.

Unsurprisingly, not everyone in the congregation agreed that this was such a good idea, yet it prompted some great conversations about the nature and purpose of Communion. After much discernment, a colleague and I were eventually granted permission to move forward, and in two subsequent football seasons, we experimented with an outreach and worship event we called Tailgate Communion. We loaded up the church van with grills, food, and beverages; found a spot on the parking deck; and threw a party for whoever wanted to join. At a set time, we cleared away the tailgating food, brought out Communion elements, and had a brief worship service. Congregation members came to support us, but we also drew a variety of fellow tailgaters interested in what we were doing. It was glorious.

Several months after the second of these worship services, an Episcopal colleague told me about a similar service in her diocese. Unaware that I had orchestrated two of these events myself, she dismissed the concept as a gimmicky act of desperation. I asked her to describe the experience. She said that some priests had set up a tent in the stadium parking lot, put on their robes, and conducted an otherwise traditional Episcopal worship service that no one seemed very interested in. "Of course they weren't interested," I responded. "If they wanted that, they would have gone to church." What made our worship service different is the way we actually *participated* in the tailgate culture and more seamlessly integrated the worshipful elements into the overall experience.

Among the participants who were not from our church and the curious passersby who asked what we were up to, the most common question I received was this: "Will you be back to do this every week?" Sadly, I had to say no—after all, I had a regular church job to attend to. But the question was telling. What we had planned as an outreach event, designed to draw people into our community of faith, ended up presenting itself as an opportunity to "be church" in an existing community. Without a doubt, the regular tailgaters at sporting events develop a genuine sense of community, primarily based on third-ring relationships. Had we invested our social capital differently, we could have become a regular spiritual presence in the midst of that community.

More and more, this is the missional frontier of our new social matrix: people of faith—we might call them *post-Christendom missionaries*—bearing witness to God's presence in all of life and engaging in faith-forming practices in existing communities and public third places. Running groups, online gaming communities, carpools, golf foursomes, and food aficionados all have the potential to be communities of faith. Dinner parties, movie nights, restaurants, pubs, coffee shops, parks, farmers' markets, gyms, and sporting events are all potential locations for spiritual formation and gospel-shaped living.

Years ago, Lesslie Newbigin and other missiologists called on the Western church to see that our own cultures are our most immediate mission fields, yet we have largely failed to answer that call. We have failed to understand ourselves as missionaries in a post-Christendom world. Our primary use of social capital is inviting people to participate in our worship services and programs because we still operate with a predominantly attractional model of church. We still operate as if one of the church's primary roles is creating community, when vibrant community exists all around us. Effective missionaries—literally, "those who are sent"—go into the world and find ways of being church in culturally relevant and compelling ways.

Inner-Ring Faith Communities

In addition to outer-ring relationships, faithful stewardship of community for networked individuals also involves investing in inner-ring relationships. Everyone's social network typically includes four to six independent groups of friends, each of which usually contain fewer than ten people. These groups tend to shift over time as our locations, life stages, interests, and shared experiences change.[20] For networked Christians in today's world, a goal should be for at least one of these inner-ring networks to be faith-based. These can take the form of small groups within a congregation, an independent missional community, or—in our increasingly post-congregational religious environment—groups of friends committed to mutual support and accountability through faith formation and spiritual practices in a variety of contexts and locations. In fact, faith-based outer-ring relationships—like those among the athletes of Sweaty Sheep—may well develop into meaningful inner-ring relationships.

The irony is, this is probably how congregations have always worked. I suspect that when people say they most value the experience of "community" in church, they are not really talking about the congregation as a whole, even when they think that they are.[21] While church members may, in fact, value the size and perceived diversity of their congregations, it is biologically and psychologically impossible to maintain strong ties with that many people. What congregations provide are environments in which to develop and nurture a relatively small number of inner-ring relationships. A congregation is not a community per se; rather, a congregation is a "basis for community" that provides a "shared context that creates the possibility for interconnections among people."[22] Congregations are essentially middle-ring clusters of inner-ring relationships. The post-Christendom shift I'm proposing is the recognition that these faith-based, inner-ring relationships can be formed and sustained in social locations other than the traditional congregational model.

The Body of Christ in the World

These different approaches to community—reinvesting our social capital in middle-ring institutions like traditional congregations or making new investments in inner- and outer-ring networks of relationships—need not be mutually exclusive. Traditional congregations can and should exist alongside new expressions of church based on the emerging social operating system of networked individualism.[23] It may be that these traditional congregations start to function more like monastic alternatives in a culture that builds community in different ways, but that's okay. God can use both traditional and emerging forms of community to grow and expand God's kingdom, which has always been the ultimate goal of Jesus' movement. Churches and church growth—and now, alternative forms of faith-based community—are always means toward that end. God's people stray from Jesus' vision when we treat these social constructs as ends in themselves.

Church membership alone does not constitute good stewardship of community, especially as traditional forms of congregational life wane. How and where we invest our social capital is an act of faith that reflects our missional priorities. There are a variety of relationships and social locations in which we have the opportunity to be church. The goal of following Jesus isn't to create self-contained communities of Christians. Rather, our calling is to live as Christ—to be the body of Christ—*in* the world.

Questions for Reflection

1. Where do you see examples of inner-ring, middle-ring, and outer-ring relationships within your community? Where do you see patterns of the "networked individualism" that characterizes our culture more broadly?
2. In what ways do you see people less inclined to "come to church" or see church as an attractional community? Given these emerging realities, how can you follow Jesus outside the walls, and "be church" elsewhere?
3. Consider Team Sweaty Sheep and the Chicago Bears pre-game Communion. What opportunities might exist for post-Christendom mission in your context?

Applications for Life Together

- Take a congregational inventory of the ways you—and your entire community—are already engaged beyond your walls. Consider new ways to embrace these assets, relationships, and connections outside of the building.
- Consider stewarding existing small-group relationships, or finding common interests and gathering around shared passions. How might your congregation embrace small-group ministry and strengthen network ties? Where have "unofficial" small groups already popped up?

9

Stewardship of Work

Called to Service

KATHLEEN A. CAHALAN

Denise is a judge. She began her professional life as a lawyer, worked in a firm, then for the U.S. attorney's office, and eventually became a judge, serving for many years in juvenile court and now at the state appellate court. She loves her work. "The career path of being a lawyer has and keeps making more of me and stretching me in ways I never imagined." What is there to love when you are confronted daily with intractable social problems? Denise loves meeting a variety of people and listening to their stories and the challenge of learning new areas of law that require research and study. Most important, she experiences being a judge as "an expression of who God made me to be." It is "deeply satisfying" work because it allows her "to express some of the gifts God gave me" such as "communication, listening, and empathy." Even though it is morally, emotionally, and personally demanding, "I get to be the human face of justice to a whole lot of people. I try to put my faith into action in my work day in how I treat people, even making hard decisions, but doing what the law requires me to do. I find my work really fulfilling."[1]

In many ways, Denise exemplifies the perfect fit of calling, work, and stewardship. As a young person she had a clear sense of being called to the law. She has worked in jobs in which she can utilize her gifts. She expresses passion for who she is and what she does. And she has found a community and a place where she can serve that makes a real difference. In this sense she is a steward of her calling as the author of 1 Peter notes, "Like good stewards of the manifold grace of God, serve one another with whatever gift each of you has received" (1 Pet. 4:10).

To discern our vocations and to shape a life in response to God's callings requires some work. It is not a one-time decision, made after high school or college graduation, as we are launched into the world. Rather, God calls us to the work of discerning our callings in all areas of life for the whole of our lives. Vocation is dynamic and relational. It is not something I passively receive from God, but rather it constitutes my response to God's invitation to live my life in relationship to God's purposes for the world. Callings are multiple and varied—Denise is also called to be a wife, mother, community advocate, and board member. God creates us with the capacity for vocation, and we are called to be good stewards of this crucial gift—our ability to respond.

If God's callings are multiple and varied from infancy to old age, then vocation cannot be confined to paid work. While *work* refers to labor, activity, exertion, and effort to produce, accomplish, or affect something, we too easily equate it with a job. The work of making our lives includes parenting, creating a neighborhood, serving on a church committee or school board, keeping a household, and visiting an elderly family member; all this is a kind of labor and effort that has purpose and needs to be valued.

For the purposes of this chapter, however, I focus mainly on work as employment. There are several ways of understanding work from both biblical and contemporary perspectives. In addition to describing these, I will share some stories from my research on vocation about how people understand their work as a calling. We found that, for some, work is a perfect fit; jobs, for others, can be a misfit or no fit at all. Young people continue to search for jobs in which they can do the work they feel called to do. And some people experience a calling to work they cannot *not* do. In conclusion, I will examine how congregations can do a better job helping people be stewards of their callings to work.

Work as Blessing and Problem

The biblical narrative has a lot to say about work. In fact, though one would not necessarily know it from the church's teachings, it has more to say about work than it does about sex. Work is filled with goodness and paradox, hope and ambiguity. The creation stories highlight work in all these ways: God works to create the natural world, animals, and human beings. God gives all these good things to human persons to care for so that they might flourish on earth (Gen. 2:15). But God also rests and establishes the Sabbath as time apart from work (vv. 1–4). After Adam and Eve sin in the garden, the ground from which human persons come from is cursed, thereby making their work difficult. Their sin against God alienates them from the very thing that bound them to God at the beginning, work as creation-making.

These ancient stories also point to the paradox of work. It is one of the primary forms of human exploitation and injustice. When the ancient Israelites were enslaved in Egypt, God was compelled by their suffering to save them: "their cry for help rose up to God. God heard their groaning, and remembered his covenant with Abraham, Isaac, and Jacob" (Exod. 2:23–24). God also demands that the people give fair treatment to their workers (see Lev. 19:13; Prov. 22:22; Jas. 5:4–14).

At the same time, work is also a blessing, given to the people in order that they might thrive and prosper. The book of Exodus describes how, during the forty years of wilderness wandering, God gave the people the work of making a sanctuary and dwelling place "[i]n accordance with all that I show you concerning the pattern" (Exod. 25:9). The pattern is delineated over eleven chapters, each beginning with the instruction, "[You] shall make . . ." (see v. 10). Furthermore, God blesses individuals with the capacity to do the work. Bezalel is blessed "with divine spirit, with ability, intelligence, and knowledge of every kind of craft"; and he is given an assistant, Oholiab. God has also "given skill to all the skillful, so that they may make all that I have commanded you" (Exod. 31:1–7). God gives important work to the people to do and the skills to get the job done.

And yet work can also be futile, as the psalmist says: "It is in vain that you rise up early / and go late to rest, / eating the bread of anxious toil" (Ps. 127:2). And life seems short and meaning-less for Job: "My days are swifter than a weaver's shuttle, / and come to their end without hope. / Remember that my life is a breath; / my eye will never again see good" (Job 7:6–7). Isaiah compares people to grass that withers and fades (Isa. 40:6–7), and one wonders whether their work does any good.

And so, work is integral to God as creator and to the pur-poses of human existence. As creatures made in God's image, our work is good and blessed when it cooperates with God's purposes for the world. God blesses us with the capacities to do good work. But when work is undertaken for our pur-poses, for self-seeking or greed, it quickly becomes abusive. We can oppress workers with unsafe labor conditions, inad-equate pay, and lack of honor. We can also abuse the gift of time by working too much, and by failing to observe the Sab-bath. Work can be meaningless drudgery that is devoid of any larger purpose—and that is true regardless of the salary.

Jobs, Careers, and Professions

Work has at least three meanings in our society. The primary reason people have worked throughout history is for *subsis-tence*: work provides the necessary materials for life, such as food, shelter, education, and health; for many of us work pro-vides money to obtain these goods. Thus we work in order to live.

Human persons also undertake work to *enhance their lives*. Work is socially valued and contributes to a person's sense of well-being, identity, and self-esteem. A career refers to work that has personal value and social standing. People aspire to do work that enhances their identity and is valued by others.

Work is also a form of *service to others*. A profession requires that a person "professes" to do work for the benefit of others. Professionals gain expert knowledge, acquire competent skills, and join a community of other practitioners, who together determine the standards and credentials for practice. Their shared practice requires a commitment to the ethics of their profession. A cardiac surgeon, for example, is committed to doing surgery for *your* health and well-being. She cannot just know about hearts, she also has to know how to cut into your chest. When she became a doctor, she took the Hippocratic Oath, by which she is required to "do no harm."

Clergy, physicians, and lawyers are the three oldest and most obvious professions in our society. But the importance of the professional ideal in North American work has meant that a set of standards and ethics now shape many kinds of work—from educators and journalists to interior designers, electricians, bankers, and business leaders. Janitors, for example, can be certified by the International Janitorial Cleaning Service Association, which claims that their "members are well educated in the field they represent, they have knowledge about the services they are going to perform and use this knowledge to inform cleaning professionals worldwide by networking."[2]

The professional ideal is a significant way that work is organized because it requires us to work for reasons beyond job (subsistence) or career (self-fulfillment). It connects work to the common good and thus is integral to a democratic society as it builds bonds of trust and loyalty among people. When I go to my accountant, I trust him to do my taxes since I don't have his expertise in tax law. Obviously, that trust can be broken. We have witnessed all too often the erosion of loyalty to professionals because too many break their promises and seek something for themselves: money, fame, and power. Just consider recent news stories about the police, U.S. senators, public school teachers, or the clergy.

Stewardship is connected to each of these ways of understanding work. When we work for subsistence, for the means to support our lives, we are involved in the stewardship of creation. All that we have been given comes from God, and stewardship calls us to care for the good of the earth (Gen. 1:28–30) as well as goods made by human hands. A steward, in the Greek version of the Hebrew Bible, is called *oikonomos*, which combines the terms "house" and "to manage." The steward was the person who served the master by caring for the household and overseeing the table. The sustenance of the household depended on good stewardship of resources in order to survive (see Gen. 43:19; 44:1–4). As stewards of creation and of the household, God calls each of us to "have dominion" and take responsibility for all that we have been given.

Having a "career" emphasizes the life-enhancing importance of work, work that is personally fulfilling and that "keeps making more of me," as Denise said. Of course if *me* is only about *ME*, then career is a selfish pursuit. To be a steward means that I care for my full becoming as a human person, that I develop God's image in me, the *imago Dei* (Gen. 1:27). As the psalmist proclaims, "what are human beings that you are mindful of them, / mortals that you care for them? / Yet you have made them a little lower than God, / and crowned them with glory and honor" (Ps. 8:4–5). When we care for ourselves by living fully into our callings, we are also stewards of God's creation.

Work as profession highlights the special skill and knowledge—the gifts we receive from God—that are required for certain kinds of work. Saint Paul explains that the Holy Spirit gives believers *charisms* that are to be used for building up the body of Christ (see Rom. 12:3–8; 1 Cor. 12:4–11; Eph. 4:11–16). *Charisms* are not for self-advancement but rather for the neighbor's good. They bear the mark of *response-ability* (I am able to respond to the other) and *responsibility* (it is my moral obligation to do so).

Because the gifts we have been given and the purposes for which we use those gifts are rooted in God's purposes, it might be more helpful to say that God gives each of us some work to do in the world; but that does not necessarily mean that God finds us a job. We make a mistake if we think that vocation amounts to having a divine job hunter. Rather, God has work for me to do in the world, and I need to discern what kind of employment or situation can best help me do that work. That journey is not easy for many people today.

Searching for the Right Fit

Many young adults struggle to find the right, or a better, fit among employment, work, and calling. Indeed, many struggle to find a position at all. Even for those who do land a suitable position, they will most likely go on to work several jobs; some will change careers or professions. After high school or college, young adults may struggle to discern a calling. Janice, a communications specialist for a large retail store, has a good job, but she is not sure about her calling: "I feel like I'm in that spot in my job right now where I'm told I'm good at it and they're moving me to some great projects but I don't know if it motivates me. . . . I don't know what my passion is. . . . I don't know what my calling is."[3]

Casey also has a good job, but unlike Janice, she knows what her calling is, and it is not in this job. Since graduating from college and earning an MBA degree, Casey has been a training coordinator, sales manager, marketing coordinator, marketing manager, and director of marketing. But when asked if marketing is her calling and her profession, she adamantly says, "No."

Casey firmly believes that her calling is to create. In college, she wanted to pursue theater, but her father dissuaded her and encouraged her to go into business. "I think my whole life I've spent hiding that piece of me, just telling myself I'm not good enough or you're never going to make a living doing that. The closest I've come is being in marketing." She stays in marketing partly because she needs to pay off student loans and partly because it taps into her creativity. At this point, she responds to her calling to create by pursuing courses in theater, writing, and drawing after working hours.

Barbara has a wonderful job in marketing, which seems like a calling, but she's unsure.

> I've come to a point several times throughout my career where I've had the urge to quit my industry and do something drastically different (go to seminary, work for a nonprofit, etc.). There have been plenty of moments when it feels my career goes against my faith. It gets to the point sometimes when I even feel guilty for liking what I do since it's so commercial.

Does this job count as a calling? Barbara wanted to know if her work mattered and had any "lasting good." She said, "I was questioning my professional direction, feeling guilty about having marketing skills (how evil!), and just didn't know where to go from there." A counselor she was seeing said something important that stuck with her. "She said, 'You know, you don't have to be working for a nonprofit to be doing something noble. Providing for your family is noble. Being a good, kind manager and co-worker is noble. There are many things you can do on a daily basis that do broader good.'" The conversation turned Barbara's singular view of worth on its head. Instead of looking for all the ways her job and career weren't worthy, she began to search for ways they were. She looked for ways, big and small, to make a positive impact on those around her every day and started focusing on those things. Barbara began to imagine her work as a calling.

Many people have to work jobs that are not a perfect fit, pay poorly, do not use their gifts, or do not conform to what they think a calling is. A job may provide subsistence but it may or may not align with a sense of calling. Sadly, many jobs today pay too little to support even an individual. When people are paid fairly, their jobs may support other callings such as raising children, providing money for education, caregiving for older parents. Some young adults hope to someday align employment, work, and calling, but they know it will take more than one job to get there.

For example, Francois emigrated from the western African nation of Burkina Faso. He earned a master's degree as a sociologist because he wanted to better understand people. When he could not find a teaching job, he decided to move to New York City where he thought a job as a sociologist seemed more likely. It didn't work out. At the age of twenty-six, Francois was left bewildered, and remembers praying, "What am I doing here? God, what do you want from me?"

He started working in a restaurant, at first washing dishes, and was embarrassed to tell his family. But the chef started having him help make desserts. He got better and eventually came to love baking; he now works as a supervisor in a food-production company. When asked about his sense of God's calling in his life, Francois says, "I define myself as a baker and a lover. As a baker because I feel like I love what I am doing. As a lover, because I am called to be a family man, called to love and watch over my family." At work, he cares about "putting out a high-quality product" and about the people he works with: "I am happy that we put a great product out there, and the employees enjoy working with me and doing a good job and loving what they are doing." And in the end, "That's why I studied sociology. I understand people need to be recognized, and that is very important in the workplace. To be seen is very important." Even though his desire to be a sociologist did not eventuate in a job, Francois found a way to do the work he loved as a sociologist in his current job.

Lauren thought her current job was only a transition until she could work toward her real calling. After college, she pursued a master's degree in theology with the expectation that she might obtain a doctorate and become a professor. After graduation, she needed a break from studying and figured she would go back to school in a year or two. She took a job at a publisher, and each year she'd say, "This year I'm going to go to graduate school." But she didn't. Finally, one day it dawned on her, "Well, maybe this is my calling. Maybe being an editor and working in publishing is where I need to be." With that realization, she felt a sense of peace, a consolation that has not left her. "This is right where I'm supposed to be, and I don't need to move out of it. I am called by God to this work, and I am called by the community." Her editing work allows her to interact with a large network of people who affirm her vocation, "I like to help people create their story and be able to tell their story." Her story, like Barbara's and Francois', points to the way a job can become the place where one discovers work he or she is called to do.[4]

Work That Cannot, *Not* Be Done

Some people have work they must do no matter what, even at a great cost. A team of sociologists, who were studying the meaning of work, found that most zookeepers have a deep sense of calling. Zookeepers described their capacity to care for animals as being "hard-wired." Because of that they have a deep passion for their work, which they see as unique and shared only among other zookeepers. Their work provides them with a high degree of meaning and purpose.

But it also entails a moral obligation that comes with a sacrifice. They work in low-paying jobs, even though they are highly educated; they work long hours at physically demanding labor, often caring for sick animals. There is not a great deal of advancement in their jobs, and, because of their commitment, zoo managers can take advantage of them. But their primary motivation to keep at the work in these jobs is a sense of calling, which surprised the sociologists. Some common remarks zookeepers were reported as saying included, "I knew this is what I was meant to do." "It's a calling for me just because my whole life I've just been interested in animals." "It's a part of who I am, and I don't know if I can explain that."[5]

For James Foley, the photojournalist who was killed by ISIS in August 2014, his calling meant giving his life for the work he had to do. Foley graduated from college in 1996, became an inner-city teacher with Teach for America in Phoenix, taught young people in the Cook County jail system, and eventually felt called to become a conflict photojournalist and report from war zones. He covered wars in Afghanistan and Libya (where he was captured and imprisoned); when the war broke out in Syria and he was preparing to leave, his mother asked him not to go. "But Mom, I've found my passion, my vocation," he said. "I have to go back. Who else is going to take those pictures and tell the stories of what these people are going through?"[6] As Christian martyrs have shown us, being called to work can cost you your life.

A Community of Stewards for Vocation

We need communities of faith to be places where people care for and help one another discern, and be good stewards of, their callings. But in fact, we found quite the opposite: most people who participated in our research do not experience their congregations as communities of calling. Jack was asked by his pastor to reflect on his calling as a financial advisor and responded by saying, "I must admit that this is the first time one of my pastors has ever asked me about what I do. Thank you for asking. I had long ago thought that anything corporate related was out of bounds for clergy to discuss or frankly they just didn't care. Happily, you have proved to be an exception to the rule."

There are at least three things pastoral leaders can do. First, we can find out what work people do and why—in all the ways discussed here. Many people reported that the conversations were the first time they had heard other people in their congregation talk about the work they do, why they do it, and why it matters. Several pastors in our project have visited people at work to get a better sense of the context, relationships, and dynamics of employment in a variety of jobs. They feel better prepared now to nurture people's sense of calling—those with the perfect fit and those who are having trouble finding it.

Second, we can value work. The way we speak about work matters, and we may not always realize the ways we demean certain kinds of work. For example, people who work in low-paying or low-skill work, such as migrant farm workers, nursing assistants, or store clerks, may find real value, meaning, and purpose in what our society deems "low" work that "no one" could possibly enjoy or find valuable. In fact, many people do. I often ask people about their work, and I have learned that, before I pass judgment, I need to let each person tell me if their work is meaningful. One young woman, who was working the makeup counter at a major department store, told me, "I love this. I know I'm not supposed to and that I should go to college, but I love color and design and helping people find what works for them." Does her work matter in our churches?

Similarly, many professional people think their work in "corporate America" is not a "calling" since it is outside of the church or not in a service profession such as teaching or health care. When asked what they need from their congregations and pastors, one person noted, "Instead of talking about how the corporate world and commercialism can work against our faith, I'd love for pastors to be mentors who can help navigate the road between the two. How can we creatively leverage our connection to big organizations and smart people to fulfill God's work? I'd love to have more discussions around that topic." If we don't know what work in corporate America is like, or assume it to be corrupt, how can we support people who feel called in that place?

Third, in addition to finding out what jobs people have and valuing their work, we can become communities of discernment. In helping college students discern a sense of calling in relationship to work, Michael Himes asks them to reflect on three questions: (1) Is what you are doing a source of joy? (2) Is it something that calls forth your gifts, engaging your abilities and talents, using them fully? (3) Is this role or work of genuine service to others and to the wider society?[7] His questions point to God's purposes in our work: our callings should bring joy and passion (not necessarily happiness), utilize our gifts, and provide us ways of giving those gifts back to God through service to others and building up the common good.

As the stories here demonstrate, there is not always a perfect fit among calling, work, and a job; or between joy, gifts, and service. In fact, many people do not have a great deal of choice about their employment. Can they be encouraged to respond to God's calling in the jobs that they do have? Inviting people to reflect together on the meaning of their work can help them discern ways to find and respond to God in that place:

- Is this a job that provides the necessary means by which I can live? Can I be a grateful steward of this work?
- Is this a job in which I can do the work to which I am called?
- If not, are there any ways that I can find to use my gifts in service of others in this job?
- Are there other places in my life—at home, at church, or in the community—where I can more fully do the work that is my calling?

In other words, we do not have to have the perfect fit in every place of employment to have a sense of work that is meaningful and good. As people move through jobs and careers, our research found that it is imperative that they have a community where they can tell their stories, hear other people's stories, reflect on their meaning, and connect them with the story of our faith. Without this most basic human support, many people will continue to feel isolated or discouraged about their work. In community, they come to realize the many ways God calls them, the importance of their work in relationship to God's purposes, and the support they need during times of transition, loss, and change at work.

Communities of discernment can help us sort out the work to which God calls us. Through this work, we participate in God's purposes for the world. We need others to help us see that our work transcends any single job that we hold, and they can help us find a context in which good work can flourish. In this sense, the community of faith can be a mentoring agent for people of all ages, companions who help us discover work that is both promise and blessing.

Questions for Reflection

1. In what ways are different vocations and gifts celebrated and shared with your faith community?
2. Are you in a job where you can be a grateful steward of your work? If not, are there ways your gifts are flourishing elsewhere?
3. How might your congregation become a community that welcomes lifelong discernment, recognizing and embracing God's gifts among you?

Applications for Life Together

- Host an educational series with an emphasis on work and/or vocation. Guiding questions might include: What does the Bible say about work? How does your particular theological tradition frame work and vocation? How do individuals in your congregation consider their work (paid or unpaid) holy?
- With key congregational leadership teams, surface gifts by using StrengthsFinder, Enneagram, spiritual-gift inventories, or other tools.

10

Stewardship of Mind

The Ascension of Our Life Together

NEAL D. PRESA

The ecclesial neighborhood I reside in is the Reformed theological tradition, and the specific address is the Presbyterian Church (U.S.A.). We Presbyterian Reformed folk pride ourselves on education, on the cultivation of the mind. There are ten theological institutions related to our General Assembly, plus another two that have a covenant agreement with the General Assembly; this is in addition to sixty-three colleges and universities that are historically related to the General Assembly. In fact, part of my denomination's storied past of ecclesiastical schisms occurred in 1741–1758, in the midst of the First Great Awakening, when the so-called Old Siders and New Siders split over the issue of educated clergy. The former group, of Scottish background, emphasized an educated clergy and ordered ministries that were doctrinally oriented. The latter emphasized revivalist techniques and, therefore, were more experiential in their orientation. While the two sides reunited in 1758, subsequent ecclesiastical divisions have (and still do) focused on this false dichotomy of mind and experience, of cognition and emotion, of our brains and of our hearts. Even the Myers-Briggs personality-type matrix assigns "T" ("thinking") and "F" ("feeling") in its assigned four-letter nomenclature.

This chapter will briefly explore the stewardship of mind in three dimensions (we're Trinitarian after all). I begin with the biblical, specifically the doxological hymn in Philippians 2:5–11, and the greatest love commandment. Next, I turn liturgical and consider the *Sursum Corda*, a historic part of Eucharistic services. Building upon this foundation, I end with the practical, considering the question: what does stewardship of mind mean for our life together as followers of Jesus Christ?

The theological framework for this discussion will be a Reformed theology of the ascension. Why the ascension? And how does the ascension of the Lord relate to the topic at hand? We live and serve after Pentecost and prior to the promised *eschaton/Parousia* of the Lord; we live in the liminal time—a between time—and space of the reality of Christ's ascension. Therefore, our commitment to being wise stewards of the mind requires an assessment of the implications of the ascension for our life now and tomorrow.

Stewardship of the Mind and the Scriptural Witness

The hymn in Philippians 2:5–11 lifts the community's attention to the notion and reality of "mind." The full context of that hymn is:

> If then there is any encouragement in Christ, any consolation from love, any sharing in the Spirit, any compassion and sympathy, make my joy complete: be of the same mind, having the same love, being in full accord and of one mind. Do nothing from selfish ambition or conceit, but in humility regard others as better than yourselves. Let each of you look not to your own interests, but to the interests of others. Let the same mind be in you that was in Christ Jesus,
>
> who, though he was in the form of God,
> did not regard equality with God
> as something to be exploited,

but emptied himself,
    taking the form of a slave,
    being born in human likeness.
And being found in human form,
    he humbled himself
    and became obedient to the point of death—
    even death on a cross.

Therefore God also highly exalted him
    and gave him the name
    that is above every name,
so that at the name of Jesus
    every knee should bend,
    in heaven and on earth and under the earth,
and every tongue should confess
    that Jesus Christ is Lord,
    to the glory of God the Father. (Phil. 2:1–11)

After commending the Philippian Christians for their faithfulness, the apostle Paul exhorts them, that—whether in his presence or in his absence—the Philippians ought to remain faithful to "live your life in a manner worthy of the gospel of Christ" (v. 27a). He then encourages them by reminding them that they are strengthened and anchored in Christ and the Holy Spirit, that they are to be of the same mind, in full accord, in one mind. While some English translations render *phroné* (v. 2, "mind") as "attitude," the term means be wise, to seek to be on the side of. Etymologically, the word's root is *phr n*, which is "mind"; in the ancient Hellenistic usage, it's the midriff or diaphragm, understood as the heart. One's brain and one's heart, while distinct, are unified in one person's being and whole existence. There is comprehensiveness in view, even in the specification of particularity. One cannot speak about following Christ in the brain but not the heart, or vice versa.

At this writing, I'm preparing to officiate my umpteenth wedding since becoming an ordained pastor. As all pastors do, we try our best, by God's grace, to prepare the couple for the day after the fancy wedding and reception . . . when getting married shifts to becoming married. In the intervening months of preparation, the couple considers their relationship, vows, and commitment. The day arrives, and there they are, standing in front of you, about to say their vows and exchange rings. Hopefully, they've considered the vows—their meaning and impact, not only at a cognitive/brain level but also at the heart level. Yes, weddings are about love (note how many weddings where the Scripture text of choice is the so-called love chapter of 1 Corinthians 13) and engaging the heart; but there's also a lot of brain there—thinking, intentional thought—so it is with marriage, and so it is with following God.

What follows the introductory verses of Philippians 2 is a comprehensive pastoral exhortation and its grounding in the comprehensive nature of Christ's service and, ultimately, of Christ's lordship. After describing what having the same mind of Christ in the Spirit looks like ("having the same love," do not be selfish or conceited, regarding others better than yourself in humility, looking out for the interests of others), the doxological hymn unfolds in verse 6. It describes the Lord's incarnation as a humble servant, entering the human condition, being obedient to God's agenda of reconciling and loving the world, "even to death on the cross." The mind that is in Christ, and which the apostle aspires will be in Christ's followers, is not merely a mental exercise or cognitive disposition; it's no less than a heart commitment, calling forth the entirety and totality of our humanity to be committed to God, to delight in God, to take on the heart agenda for the life of the world.

The apostle is not an Apollinarianist (Apollinarianism is that ancient heresy that viewed Christ as having a divine mind only and a human body with a lower soul; this teaching was rejected by the First Council of Constantinople in 381 CE), giving more weight to Christ's heavenly existence than his earthly existence, or claiming that Christ's mind was about only heavenly things. Rather, the doxological hymn portrays the oneness, the sameness, of the Lord's heavenly/earthly, divine/human commitments: being God though not seeing equality with God as something to be exploited. The Lord Jesus is completely and totally for God *and* for humanity, taking on the heart and mind of the former in order to reconcile, love, and serve the latter.

The Lord Jesus' total commitment to God's heart agenda finds expression in God's own commitment to exalt Jesus Christ. God's exaltation of Jesus Christ is comprehensive, calling forth all nations to confess "that Jesus Christ is Lord, / to the glory of God" (v. 11).

This Philippians 2 hymn confesses and describes what constitutes having "the same mind . . . in you that was in Christ Jesus" (v. 5). The hymn is speaking about matters of the heart. This ancient confession, sung by the gathered worshiping assembly, directs the whole community's heart to the exalted Lord, the One who is ascended; the One whose whole body was incarnated; who was a servant God-man, died on the cross, and rose from the grave. His total being is ascended, and, in his exaltation, our hearts are, likewise, joined to his through the presence and power of the Holy Spirit. I'll have more to say about the significance of our union in Christ below. What's important now is that, in specifying the particularities of what it means to take on the mind of Christ, the doxological hymn in Philippians 2 calls forth the whole people of God—in their whole personhood, as a whole community—to be united to the fullness of God—the Father, the Son, the Holy Spirit—in their worship and in their witness. In short, to take on the "mind of Christ" is to have the entirety of mind, body, and heart anchored in and animated toward the very life of God, whose life in Christ was for the redemption and reconciliation of the world.

Beyond Philippians 2, the comprehensiveness and totality of what constitutes "mind" commitment can be seen in Old Testament and Gospel passages that relate the greatest love commandment. The *Shema* of Deuteronomy 6:5 states: "You shall love the LORD your God with all your heart, and with all your soul, and with all your might." Three instances in the Gospels mention the first love commandment:

- "He said to him, 'You shall love the Lord your God with all your heart, and with all your soul, and with all your mind'" (Matt. 22:37).
- "[Y]ou shall love the Lord your God with all your heart, and with all your soul, and with all your mind, and with all your strength" (Mark 12:30).
- "He answered, 'You shall love the Lord your God with all your heart, and with all your soul, and with all your strength and with all your mind'" (Luke 10:27a).

The LXX (Septuagint) version of Deuteronomy renders the Hebrew word for "might" (*meod*) as *dynámeos* ("power" or "strength"). Only in Matthew's rendition is the word "strength" left out; whereas "mind" is retained in all references to the first commandment in the Gospels. The word "mind" (*dianoia*) denotes one's thoughts, feelings, desires, or disposition. To speak of mind is necessarily to speak of heart, which entails the soul, which requires your might or your strength. In other words, *mind* is a synecdochical relationship—as used in Scripture—interrelating with other parts of our being, including them in it, and it with them. For a common synecdoche, the expression "All hands on deck" colloquially means that everyone should be involved in the project; that it's urgent to drop everything, and everyone should pitch in. But its literal meaning also applies: as everyone pitches in, everyone's hands will literally be involved in the effort.

Mind, as synecdoche in Scripture, denotes comprehensiveness and totality. *Mind*, as part of the first love commandment, expresses the whole commitment of the human being and the call for the whole inhabited earth to love God. The embodiment of this comprehensive and total love is Jesus Christ, whose love for both God and humanity was preeminent. We can't split Christ into bits and pieces; Christ's whole personhood in his divine/human nature, in his divine/human will, in his being as the God-man, in being the Son of God and the Son of Man, was committed to God and to the redemption and reconciliation of the world. This total commitment of love to God and love to neighbor is what is called forth from those who are redeemed and reconciled to God and to other human beings.

To exercise stewardship of mind, then, is to be a faithful, trusted, and trustworthy custodian of your whole self. This is reflected in the opening words of the Heidelberg Catechism (1563): "What is your only comfort, in life and in death? That I belong—body and soul, in life and in death—not to myself but to my faithful Savior, Jesus Christ."[1] To be a steward of mind is to exercise wisdom, because in Scripture, wisdom is the use of knowledge and understanding toward fearing (read "honoring") God, thanking God, and loving God. The apostle Paul exhorted, "So, whether you eat or drink, or whatever you do, do everything for the glory of God" (1 Cor. 10:31). St. Irenaeus, in the second century, famously observed, "The glory of God is a human being alive." Therefore, being a wise steward of mind is to attend to the matters of the heart, the body, and, thus, our whole being, so that loving God and loving neighbor is our mission statement in life, the same heart-mind agenda that animated Jesus Christ, and what he calls us to do in the power of the Holy Spirit.

Stewardship of Mind and Our Liturgical Life

It's been standard fare at the beginning of meetings or a gathering to offer the first part of the *Sursum Corda* (from the Latin, "lift up your hearts"), by saying, "The Lord be with you," to which the gathered assembly responds, "And also with you." It turns out, though, that these words are more than an ancient statement meaning, "Hush up! Let's begin." In fact, the remainder of the *Sursum Corda* is key to completing the theology and purpose of this responsive litany:

> One: The Lord be with you.
> **All: And also with you.**
> One: Lift up your hearts.
> **All: We lift them to the Lord.**
> One: Let us give thanks to the Lord our God.
> **All: It is right to give our thanks and praise.**

While the customary usage of the "Lord be with you. / And also with you." combination is a quick ecclesiastical alternative to the hackneyed conversational starter "How are you? / Fine, thank you. And how are you?" the fullness of the *Sursum Corda*, as it occurs within the Eucharistic liturgy, is intended to express the worshiping assembly's desire to lean upon the presence of the Lord at the Table, to recognize and affirm the Lord's necessary presence to make what appears to be an ordinary meal an extraordinary one, and to confess that through the presence and power of the Holy Spirit, we are united to the ascended Christ. Staying with only the first half of the *Sursum Corda* focuses our attention on the Lord's presence among us. Proceeding to complete the *Sursum Corda* orients us to the Lord's present absence and the Lord's absent presence: God is both here and not here; God is among us, even as God is seated at the right hand of God, even (as we confess in the Creed) as we also are being united into God's ascended life by virtue of the union we have with God through the Holy Spirit.

For John Calvin, the indwelling Spirit of Christ (his divine nature) brought the soul of the believer to heaven to be in union with Christ's glorified body (his human nature), while imparting the presence of that same glorified body to the believer. In Calvin's mind, to speak of receiving the substance of Christ's body was to speak of the body's presence in power and efficacy (*virtute, efficacia*).[2] Thus, those of us who belong to the Presbyterian Reformed theological traditions can truly say we eat of the body of Christ and we drink of the blood of Christ, which means we are so united to the ascended Christ by the uniting work of the Holy Spirit that we sacramentally and really participate in the life of Christ. To take on the mind of Christ is not *imitatio Christi*; it is truly internalizing the mind and heart of Christ in the union we have with Christ, a union whose fulcrum and pivot is the presence and power of the Holy Spirit. It's no wonder that Calvin saw in the *Sursum Corda*, not a mere greeting, but the action of the Holy Spirit in lifting (read: uniting in communion) the gathered assembly into the heavenly realm where the ascended Christ dwells.

Practical Implications

"Stewardship of the mind," as we have seen, involves more than merely attending to our mental faculties, our personal enrichment, or book learning. It certainly involves those things: we ought to attend to careful biblical exegesis; we should know our systematic theologies and bring understanding of contextual Christian history, read the classics, and so on. But being a steward of the mind is to engage our whole being with the whole body of Christ in wisely living out God's call upon the people of God in every time and in every place to love the Lord with all of our heart, soul, mind, and strength, and to love one another as Christ has loved us.[3] To be wise stewards of our minds is to take on the mind of Christ, which means being united to the ascended Christ, which means being in and living with the power and presence of the Holy Spirit. Or to put it in Pauline terms,

> I appeal to you therefore, brothers and sisters, by the mercies of God to present your bodies as a living sacrifice, holy and acceptable to God, which is your spiritual worship. Do not be conformed to this world, but be transformed by the renewing of your minds, so that you may discern what is the will of God—what is good and acceptable and perfect. (Rom. 12:1–2)

Stewarding the mind is best done in community. This is the primary locus of worship, where the people of God attend to the ministry of Word and Sacrament. These two marks of the Church—preaching and Sacrament—were recognized by the Reformers as the primary means by which and through which the Lord shapes the hearts and minds of the community. But it is not just in worship; it is in service and mission.[4] When we serve together, pray together, feast together, we take on more and more the mind of the ascended Christ as the Spirit of Christ animates and anchors us to the heart and mind of God.

Because stewarding the mind on this side of heaven is done within the purview of the ascended Christ, believers live and serve in the constant paradox of the absent presence and present absence of the Lord Christ.[5] We can say as believers, "Christ is not here. Christ is here." without contradiction or double-speak. One common way this is expressed is: "The Lord be with you / And also with you / Lift up your hearts. / We lift them to the Lord." Sound familiar? That is what the church confesses in the full *Sursum Corda*.

To doubly confess the Lord's presence in absence and absence in presence is to live and serve in a healthy tension. What Karl Barth called the "in-between times"[6] or Sang Hyun Lee's "liminality,"[7] the *hic et nunc* (here and now) means dwelling in the tension of certainty and mystery, of authority and freedom. To live with certainty is to know and trust in the promises of God, in sure confidence that God is true and trustworthy, that the gospel is indeed "the power of God for salvation" (Rom. 1:16).

We live with this tension of certainty and mystery every single day. My wife and I are raising two wonderful sons—chauffeuring them to sports activities, accompanying them on Boy Scout events, paying for music lessons, praying with them daily, teaching them manners, and all the rest that goes with parenting. But all of it is by God's grace, because we are also aware that our years of parenting do not guarantee a certain outcome. They will and do make their own decisions; and there will come a day when they leave the roost, and they will make choices, hopefully guided by some of the meager wisdom we impart. Here's certainty and mystery at play. For those of us who preach and have to share the Word from the pulpit to our congregations, there's an interplay of what the preacher has carefully crafted in her study, and what impact that sermon will have on her hearers at the greeting time in the narthex: "Thank you, Pastor Mary, that was a sermon that blessed me," or "Pastor John, I didn't like that message."

At the same time, we live in the mystery of God, what God is doing in our midst, or, in Pauline terms once again, in that great benediction: "Now to him, who by the power at work within us is able to accomplish abundantly far more than all we can ask or imagine . . ." (Eph. 3:20). When we proclaim the good news of God in Christ through the Holy Spirit, we are certain of God's decisive work at the cross, at the empty tomb, at the ascension; this is the gospel. At the same time, we don't know the mechanics or time when and how the Spirit of Christ is working in the minds and hearts of people to transform them, to bend hearts toward their Maker, the Lord who is making all things new, even when our eyes strain to catch glimpses.

Living in the tension of the ascension reminds us of what is at stake in being stewards of the mind. Navigating and discerning in the midst of certainty/mystery requires a habit of the mind/heart that is humble but confident. This means being a faithful witness of what we have received—the traditions of the faith—while humbly deferring to what the Spirit of Christ might be doing with that witness, even as we receive testimony from others. The hard but necessary work of ecumenical dialogues and interreligious/interfaith engagements is an expression of this. To be a serious participant and conversation partner in such encounters requires a deep tethering in what you believe; it's not relativistic, or discussing the lowest common denominator while eliding the distinct differences between ecclesial traditions, let alone non-Christian faith communities. Rather, it is honest, full engagement with what we have come to know and believe with confidence, while humbly being open to the gifts of conversation partners who bear the image of God and with whom and through whom we discover who our neighbor is.

In 2013, I had the privilege of representing the Presbyterian Church (U.S.A.) as moderator of the 220th General Assembly, on a trip to Lebanon. Our delegation visited Kab Elias (meaning "grave of Elijah"), the third largest city in the Beqaa Valley. There are mosques alongside Christian churches; and in this predominantly Muslim area, there is peaceful coexistence of Christian and Muslim neighbors.

This was apparent at a school operated by the National Evangelical Synod of Syria and Lebanon, our partner church in the region. The Evangelical Synod educates elementary-school-aged kids who are both Christian and Muslim; in fact, many of the students are driven long distances because both Christian and Muslim families alike know of the great education the school provides, an education that is outwardly grounded in the values of being Christian.

The church is at its best when the proper balance of freedom and authority is maintained. To have ultimate freedom is a nihilistic existence, almost like the closing word of the Old Testament book of Judges: "In those days there was no king in Israel; all the people did what was right in their own eyes" (Jdg. 21:25). The other extreme—to exercise full authority—is to be cultic, oppressive, and enforcing rules and regulations to the point of stifling human freedom in God's grace. Living in the proper perspective of the ascension is to live in the middle tension, dignifying both the individual, creative support, and dignifying the tradition of the cloud of witnesses; or to put it in the wise words of the Reformed motto, "reformed and always being reformed according to the Word of God."

Stewardship of the mind is the lifelong call to put on the mind, and, therefore, heart of Christ. It is to have our minds committed to what the Lord was committed to: loving God and loving neighbor. The pivot and fulcrum of that ministry is the Spirit of the ascended Christ, who works in, through, and upon us, primarily in community, through the community's worship, mission, discipleship, and service. In its personal and communal dimensions, attending to the stewardship of the mind is to engage the wholeness of our being, the totality of the body of Christ, for the life of the world. It can be no other, because stewarding the mind is a significant expression of the giving of God's whole self for the reconciliation and redemption of the whole creation.

Questions for Reflection

1. How might you explore ways to embrace stewardship of mind, particularly in relation to your mental faculties?
2. In what ways might you explore opportunities to stewardship your mind in ways that might reconnect, or realign mind with heart, soul, and strength?
3. Given the chapter's emphasis on wholeness, in what ways does your congregation promote holistic well-being? In what ways does your congregation encourage the holistic well-being of the surrounding community?

Applications for Life Together

- Consider engaging in interfaith/interreligious partnership or dialogue. Note that the chapter suggests interfaith or ecumenical work best comes from "a deep tethering in what you believe" as opposed to approaches focusing on "the lowest common denominator."
- Embrace the Lord's Supper as a time of being united with Christ's body as well as one another. Consider study, new practices, or liturgies that emphasize this Eucharist as an opportunity for community wholeness.

Biblical Texts and Preaching Themes

As often as possible, Scripture references are drawn from suggestions in the chapter itself. Many more possibilities exist than those provided, but I pray these may serve as a helpful guide for further study and discussion.

1. Stewardship of Time: Clocks, Calendars, and Cathedrals

- *Genesis 1–2*: God deems rest a holy and necessary act when God rests on the seventh day. As we seek to be good stewards of our time, we must strive to include both times of creation (work) and holy rest.
- *Psalm 90*: The psalm invites us to consider distinctions between *kairos* and *chronos*, the fullness of God's time and our chronological time. Consider also God's vastness and our smallness in a way that frees us from inflated self-perceptions and addiction to overwork.

2. Stewardship of Life at Its End:
"Receive the Sign of the Cross"

- *Psalm 13*: In our anger and pain, we are free to cry out to God in lament. Our laments in and of themselves are acts of great faith, as we call on God to remember God's people and proclaim God's faithfulness in the midst of grief. We also find comfort in knowing that in Jesus, God suffers alongside us.
- *Luke 24:13–25*: As we seek to accompany one another, we enter into one another's life stories of joy, anger, hope, and lament. In the Road to Emmaus story, we find that Christ too enters into our life stories, into our joy as well as our pain.
- *Romans 14:1–8*: Belonging to Christ means, also, that we belong to others in the body of Christ. Dependency is not a state to be feared; rather it is a state of belonging to a community. We are called to care for and receive care from one another.

3. Stewardship of Money and Finances:
Practicing Generosity as a Way of Life

- *Deuteronomy 15:7–11*: Concern for the well-being of our neighbors is central to our identity as people of God. We are to respond to the needs of our neighbors with generosity. In this way, stewardship is not merely a private spiritual practice between us and God, but a broader issue of justice, deeply connected to our life in God and our call to respond to neighbors in God's love.
- *Matthew 19:16–30*: While possessions and money are not evil in themselves, our culture often cultivates an environment in which our possessions possess us. Being stewards and disciples of Christ, we are called to use our possessions and wealth to love and serve God and neighbors, trusting that our identity is already secure in Christ.
- *Matthew 21:33–46*: Stewards are called to nurture, not just manage. We can nurture our gifts, generosity, and sense of gratitude as we seek to be better stewards of all that we have and all that we are, and as we live more fully into the life and promises of God.

- *1 John 3:11–24*: God is love, and God abides in us; we are called to share in God's life by loving our neighbors. This love takes a concrete form in generosity and stewardship of wealth and possessions, an outpouring of generosity in response to God's generosity toward us.

4. Stewardship of Technology: Digital Gifts

- *Psalm 24*: All that we have belongs to God, for it is God who creates. Therefore, all we have, including technology, should be used for God's glory and for participating in God's kingdom.
- *John 13:31–35*: If we "ponder technology in the presence of Jesus," a central question becomes how our technology usage helps or hinders us from loving one another with Christ's love.
- *Romans 8:1–17*: As people set free from the bondage of sin and death and called into the new life of the Spirit, we should pay attention to the formative power of technology on our lives. Our technology use should be centered on the promise of our freedom in Christ, and our stewardship of technology should reflect the life-giving power of the Gospel.

5. Stewardship of Privilege: Toward the Stewardship of Incarnation

- *Acts 2*: The Spirit creates diversity as it is poured out upon the apostles at Pentecost. Thus, contrary to our tendencies to value certain incarnational realities above others, diversity is in fact a gift from God that should be celebrated. As we seek to be stewards of incarnation, we are called to live into God's celebration of diversity and to dismantle systems that keep us from fully embracing this reality.
- *Acts 6:1–7*: In the face of systemic inequality, the apostles choose to appoint new leadership from the oppressed culture to address the issue. Here we find a model for dismantling harmful structures, thereby practicing a "stewardship of incarnation" as opposed to a "stewardship of privilege."

- *1 Corinthians 12*: We are called to recognize and celebrate diversity within the Body of Christ and also to stand in solidarity with members who are oppressed. To be stewards of incarnation, however, we may need to go further than solidarity and seek to change the system entirely.
- *Revelation 13*: Systems of privilege and oppression are idolized in society, like the first beast in John's revelation. Instead of imitating harmful systems as the people imitate the beast, we are called to recognize privilege as idolatry and instead embrace God's reality of love and justice for all people.

6. Stewardship of Spirit: Stewarding Spiritual Gifts

- *Isaiah 11:2–3*: In our baptism, the Spirit anoints us with gifts, equipping us to love God and neighbor as we participate in the life of God.
- *Mark 12:28–34; Deuteronomy 6:4–5*: We are to love God *and* neighbor holistically: with all our heart, mind, soul, and strength.
- *Romans 5:1–15*: In baptism, God's love is poured into our hearts through the Spirit. As we put our hope in the promises of sharing in God's glory, we are called to love our neighbors with God's love, sharing our own gifts with the world.
- *1 Corinthians 12*: The Spirit pours out a diversity of gifts among the body of Christ. In order to steward these gifts well, we must recognize the spectacular diversity of gifts among the body, affirm the value in each, and share our own gifts out of gratitude and abundance for the sake of the whole.

7. Stewardship of Body: On Flesh

- *Genesis 1–2*: God creates humans—including our bodies—and declares them "very good." God makes us to live *in* the world, delighting in the rest of creation, not in a separate spiritual realm.

- *Psalm 139*: God creates us and knows us, knitting together our bodies and the intricacies of our human existence.
- *Matthew 1:18–25; Luke 2:1–20; John 1:1–18* (Jesus' birth): God takes on flesh, entering into our realities by becoming human. God knows the complexities, joys, and sufferings of what it means to live as fully human.
- *John 9:1–12*: Jesus cares about our bodily needs, healing people of physical disease, estrangement, and more. Jesus embraces the earthiness of our reality, using elements like spit and dirt to bring healing. We too are called to pay attention to the bodies of our neighbors as we seek to love and serve.

8. Stewardship of Community:
Investing Social Capital as an Act of Faith

- *Matthew 28:16–20*: The mission of the church is not to function as a social club, but instead to be sent into the world and surrounding communities, sharing Christ's love and "making disciples of all nations."
- *Acts 2*: At Pentecost, the creative Spirit equips us with a diversity of gifts with which to love and serve communities both near and far in Christ's name.
- *Romans 12*: In our life together, we are called to love and serve one another, showing hospitality to strangers and bearing one another's burdens. Paul's exhortation applies whether our community dwells within the walls of a church, finds itself in the broader community, or takes shape online.

9. Stewardship of Work: Called to Service

- *Genesis 2*: As God gives Adam and Eve creative roles to work and care for the garden, God too calls us to be co-creators in God's world.
- *Leviticus 19:13; Proverbs 22:22; James 5:4–14*: God cares about justice and fairness in our work with others. God calls

us to strive for justice in the midst of our daily activity as well as work for justice more broadly. God does not abandon those who are oppressed.

- *1 Peter 4:1–11*: We have each been given gifts to work for goodness and wholeness in our communities. All that we have should be used for love of neighbor.
- *Romans 12:3–8; 1 Corinthians 12:4–11; Ephesians 4:11–16*: As the body of Christ, we have been given a diversity of gifts, all of which are of value to God. Our individual gifts should always be used for the sake of the broader community in the world God loves. This multitude of gifts leads to a multitude of vocations, all of which are holy when lived in service to our neighbors.

10. Stewardship of Mind: The Ascension and Our Life Together

- *Deuteronomy 6:5 (also Matthew 22:37; Mark 12:30; Luke 10:27a)*: We are called to love God with all of our being: heart, soul, mind, and strength. Loving God is an all-encompassing experience that requires stewardship of our whole selves. God is always drawing us toward wholeness as we give of all that we are.
- *Matthew 26:26–30; Mark 14:22–25; Luke 22:14–23; 1 Corinthians 11:23–26*: In the Lord's Supper, we are fully united with Christ and with one another as members of Christ's body. Through the Spirit's presence in the sacrament, we are made of one mind and heart with Christ and are sent into the world to be stewards of Christ's love that fills the entirety of our being.
- *Philippians 2:5–11*: To be in the same mind as Christ is to have the same love as Christ; the two cannot be separated. We are to live out of Christ's love and humility. Being good stewards of Christ's love results in a radical outpouring of love to the neighbor as we are all called to participate in the unity and fullness of God's life.

Notes

Introduction

1. *Oxford English Dictionary*, s.v. "steward," last modified March 2016, accessed May 8, 2016, http://www.oed.com.luthersem.idm.oclc.org/view/Entry/190087?rskey=R0Exh3&result=1.

Chapter 1: Time

1. Walter Hickey, "The Truth about Jeff Bezos' Amazing 10,000-Year Clock," *Business Insider* (August 12, 2013), accessed April 21, 2016, http://www.businessinsider.com/everything-you-need-to-know-about-jeff-bezos-amazing-10000-year-clock-2013-8.

2. Ibid.

3. Robert L. Leahy, "How Big a Problem Is Anxiety?" *Psychology Today* (April 30, 2008), accessed April 21, 2016, https://www.psychologytoday.com/blog/anxiety-files/200804/how-big-problem-is-anxiety.

4. Mark R. Robertson, "500 Hours of Video Uploaded to YouTube Every Minute [Forecast]," *ReelSEO* (November 13, 2015), accessed April 21, 2016, http://www.reelseo.com/hours-minute-uploaded-youtube/.

5. James Surowiecki, "The Cult of Overwork," *The New Yorker* (January 27, 2014), accessed April 21, 2016, http://www.newyorker.com/magazine/2014/01/27/the-cult-of-overwork.

6. Frank Chung and AAP, "The Country Working Itself to Death," *news.com.au* (March 7, 2015), accessed April 21, 2016, http://www.news.com.au/finance/work/at-work/the-country-working-itself-to-death/news-story/5c29cd052ce1b58e14247fc5f349163b.

7. Ross Luippold, "Jim Gaffigan Thinks Phone Photos Are Ruining America's Children, He Tells Conan," *Huffington Post* (April 13, 2012),

157

accessed April 21, 2016, http://www.huffingtonpost.com/2012/04/13/
jim-gaffigan-thinks-phone-photos-ruin-children_n_1423919.html.

8. Mark Mancina, Jay Rifkin, and Lebo M., "He Lives in You," *The Lion King* (Walt Disney Music Company, ©1994–2004).

9. Ibid., Tim Rice, "The Circle of Life."

10. Anne Lamott, *Bird by Bird: Some Instructions on Writing and Life* (New York: Anchor Books, 1995), 170.

11. Max De Pree, *Leadership Jazz: The Essential Elements of a Great Leader* (New York: Random House, 2009), 241–42.

Chapter 2: Life at Its End

1. Stephen P. Bouman, *From the Parish for the Life of the World* (Minneapolis: Augsburg Fortress, 2000), 51–52.

2. Medicare and other insurance plans generally define activities of daily living to include personal hygiene, dressing, eating, maintaining continence, and transferring oneself from sitting to standing or from chair to bed.

3. This does not mean that we acknowledge no differences between, for instance, a caregiver and someone who is cognitively impaired (and therefore unable to make appropriate decisions about where to live, what to eat, etc.). It does mean that we treat others with kindness and respect no matter what their level of impairment or need.

4. Martin Luther, "Heidelberg Disputation," *Luther's Works* 31:39–70, ed. Jaroslav Pelikan et al. (Philadelphia: Fortress Press; St. Louis: Concordia Publishing House, 1955–).

5. Carl R. Trueman, *Luther on the Christian Life: Cross and Freedom* (Wheaton, IL: Crossway, 2015), 63.

6. Douglas John Hall, "'We Are Not Alone': Reflections on 'Atonement,'" *Touchstone* 31, no. 2 (June 2013): 30 (emphasis original).

7. Because I outline three practices and three beliefs, readers may conclude that I intend to "key" each belief to a practice. In fact, I think each practice embodies elements of all three beliefs.

8. See John Swinton, *Raging with Compassion: Pastoral Responses to the Problem of Evil* (Grand Rapids: Eerdmans, 2007), 90–129. See also, "'Why Me, Lord?': Practicing Lament at the Foot of the Cross" in *Living Well and Dying Faithfully: Christian Practices for End-of-Life Care*, ed. John Swinton and Richard Payne (Grand Rapids: Eerdmans, 2009), 107–38, where Swinton has drawn the practice of lament and the theology of the cross into conversation with each other.

9. *Raging with Compassion*, 104.

10. Swinton cites Ann Weems, *Psalms of Lament* (Louisville, KY: Westminster John Knox, 1995) and thanks colleague Bill Gaventa for offering the structure for writing that follows.

11. Martin Rinckart, "Now Thank We All Our God," tr. Catherine Wink-worth, *Glory to God: the Presbyterian Hymnal* (Louisville, KY: Westminster John Knox, 2013), #643.

12. Anne Lamott, *Help, Thanks, Wow: Three Essential Prayers* (New York: Penguin, 2012).

13. Eric Smith, "Wild Goose Day Two: Embodiment," *Patheos* (blog), August 10, 2013, http://www.patheos.com/blogs/faithforward /2013/08/wild-goose-day-two-embodiment/.

14. Richard Lischer, *Stations of the Heart: Parting with a Son* (New York: Knopf, 2013), 118–19.

15. "StoryCorps", https://storycorps.org/great-questions/.

16. Robert G. LaFavi and Marcia H. Wessels, "Life Review in Pastoral Counseling: Background and Efficacy for Use with the Terminally Ill," *The Journal of Pastoral Care & Counseling* 57, no. 3 (September 2003): 281–92.

17. Richard Morgan, *Remembering Your Story: Creating Your Own Spiritual Autobiography*, 4th ed. (Nashville: Upper Room Books, 2009). Dan Wakefield, *The Story of Your Life: Writing a Spiritual Autobiography* (Boston: Beacon Press, 1990).

18. *Peace at the Last: Visitation with the Dying* (Minneapolis: Augsburg Fortress, 2016).

19. "Welcome to Baptism," *Evangelical Lutheran Worship* (Minneapolis: Augsburg Fortress, 2006), 232f. The Roman Catholic rite may be viewed at http://www.catholicnh.org/assets/Documents/Catholic Faith/RCIA/AcceptanceAndWelcoming.pdf.

20. *Peace at the Last*, 40–41.

21. Richard Lischer, "We Have Seen the Lord," *The Christian Century*, March 17, 1999, 307.

Chapter 3: Money and Finances

1. Robert Wuthnow, *Poor Richard's Principle: Recovering the American Dream through the Moral Dimension of Work, Business, and Money* (Princeton, NJ: Princeton University Press, 1996), 140.

2. Jaroslav Pelikan, "Stewardship of Money in the Early Church," *Good and Faithful Servant*, ed. Anthony Scott (Crestwood: St. Vladimir's Seminary Press).

3. Janet T. and Philip D. Jamieson, *Ministry and Money: A Practical Guide for Pastors* (Louisville, KY: Westminster John Knox, 2009), 22–23.

4. "Learning by Giving," accessed May 5, 2016, http://www.learningby givingfoundation.org/.

5. Indiana University Lilly Family School of Philanthropy, *Giving USA 2016: The Annual Report on Philanthropy for the Year 2015* (Giving USA Foundation, 2016), 59, available at http://givingusa.org.

6. Melanie McKitrick, J. Landres, Mark Ottoni-Wilhelm, and Cynthia

Hayat, "Connected to Give: Faith Communities" (Los Angeles: Jumpstart, 2013), 6, available at http://connectedtogive.org/reports/.

7. The Saguaro Seminar, "2006 Social Capital Community Survey," Harvard Kennedy School, available at https://www.hks.harvard.edu/saguaro/measurement/2006sccs.htm.

8. Brandon Vaidyanathan and Patricia Snell, "Motivations for and Obstacles to Religious Financial Giving," *Sociology of Religion* 72, no. 2 (2011): 189–214.

9. Christian Smith and Hilary Davidson, *The Paradox of Generosity* (New York: Oxford University Press, 2014).

10. Mark Allan Powell, *Giving to God: The Bible's Good News about Living a Generous Life* (Grand Rapids, MI: Eerdmans, 2006).

11. Moses Maimonides, "Laws Concerning Gifts to the Poor," in *The Perfect Gift: The Philanthropic Imagination in Poetry and Prose*, ed. Amy A. Kass (Bloomington: Indiana University Press, 2002), 125–26.

12. Robert D. Lupton, *Toxic Charity* (New York: HarperOne, 2011); Brian Fikkert and Steve Corbett, *When Helping Hurts: How to Alleviate Poverty without Hurting the Poor . . . and Yourself* (Chicago: Moody, 2014).

13. In developing this theology of Christian philanthropy, I want to acknowledge the foundational tenets that originated in the conversations and teaching of Craig Dykstra in Lake Institute on Faith and Giving's Executive Certificate of Religious Fundraising (ECRF).

Chapter 4: Technology

1. In receiving Paul's permission to share his story, he reported that he's become a sort of "sudden cardiac arrest" (SCA) evangelist. When a person collapses and is experiencing an SCA, time is crucial. Only a rapid response can save lives, including calling 911, administering CPR, and treating with an automated external defibrillator (AED). In the United States alone, SCA accounts for more than 350,000 deaths each year.

2. Michael Lindvall, "Living in a Material World," *The Christian Century*, July 13, 2010, 10.

3. Charles R. Lane, *Ask, Thank, Tell: Improving Stewardship Ministry in Your Congregation* (Minneapolis, Fortress, 2006), 21–22.

4. Miroslav Volf, *Free of Charge: Giving and Forgiving in a Culture Stripped of Grace* (Grand Rapids: Zondervan, 2005), 84.

5. Ibid., 36.

6. Quotation attributed to McLuhan's colleague John Culkin. For Culkin's explanation, see John M. Culkin, "A Schoolman's Guide to Marshall McLuhan," *Saturday Review* (March 18, 1967), 51–53, 71–72.

7. See Abraham Harold Maslow, *The Psychology of Science* (New York: Harper & Row, 1966), x.

8. "Distracted Walking Injuries on the Rise; 52 Percent Occur at home," National Safety Council, June 17, 2015, accessed December 23, 2016, http://www.nsc.org/Connect/NSCNewsReleases/Lists/Posts/Post.aspx?ID=15.

9. Elizabeth Drescher and Keith Anderson, *Click 2 Save: The Digital Ministry Bible* (Harrisburg, PA: Morehouse, 2012), 22.

10. Ibid.

11. danah boyd, *It's Complicated: The Social Lives of Networked Teens* (New Haven: Yale University Press, 2014), 90.

12. Ibid., 91.

13. John Calvin, *Institutes of Christian Religion*, vol. 1, ed. John T. McNeill (Philadelphia: Westminster Press, 1960), 108.

14. Craig Detweiler, *iGods: How Technology Shapes Our Spiritual and Social Lives* (Grand Rapids, MI: Brazos Press, 2013), 3–4.

15. Lance Pape, "Talking about Money in the Presence of Jesus: Biblical Hermeneutics and the Call for Topical Preaching," *Practical Matters Journal* (October 1, 2014), http://wp.me/p6QAmj-5c.

16. Chris Ridgeway, "How to Preach about Technology (Don't)," *Leadership Journal* (July 8, 2014), http://www.christianitytoday.com/le/2014/july-online-only/how-to-preach-about-technology-dont.html.

17. Pape, "Talking about Money in the Presence of Jesus."

18. Evangelical Lutheran Church in America, *Genetics, Faith and Responsibility* (Chicago: ELCA, 2011), 14.

19. Ibid., 10.

20. Ibid., 2.

Chapter 5: Privilege

1. Ronnie Goldstein and Guy G. Stroumsa, "The Greek and Jewish Origins of Docetism: A New Proposal." *Zeitschrift Für Antikes Christentum* 10, no. 3 (2006): 423–41.

2. Nestor Medina, "Transgressing Theological Shibboleths: Culture as Locus of Divine (Pneumatological) Activity," *Pneuma* 36 (2014): 432–46.

3. Ted Greenberg, "'English-Only' Contract Stirs Controversy at N. J. School." *NBC10: News* (July 17, 2009), accessed May 12, 2016, http://www.nbcphiladelphia.com/news/local/English-Only-Guidelines-Stirs-Controversy-at-Vineland-School.html. See also T. R. Reid, "Spanish at School Translates to Suspension," *Washington Post* (December 9, 2005), accessed May 12, 2016, http://www.washingtonpost.com/wp-dyn/content/article/2005/12/08/AR2005120802122.html. These are only a few of many examples.

4. Lucy Westcott, "Muslim Student Kicked Off Southwest Airlines

Flight for Speaking Arabic," *Newsweek* (April 19, 2016), http://www.newsweek.com/muslim–student–southwest–airlines–arabic –449598.

5. Mike McPhate, "Discrimination by Airbnb Hosts Is Widespread, Report Says," *The New York Times* (December 11, 2015), http://nyti.ms/1Z3HPa9.

6. J. Kameron Carter, *Race: A Theological Account* (New York: Oxford University Press, 2008), 351–53.

7. Carolyn Browning Helsel, "Sermon on Philippians 2" (unpublished sermon, Austin Presbyterian Theological Seminary, April 25, 2016).

8. Michael Battle, *Ubuntu: I in You and You in Me* (New York: Seabury Books, 2009), 2.

9. Treva B. Lindsey, "Black No More: Skin Bleaching and the Emergence of New Negro Womanhood Beauty Culture," *Journal of Pan African Studies* 4 (2011): 97–116; Tracey Owens Patton, "Hey Girl, Am I More than My Hair? African American Women and Their Struggles with Beauty, Body Image, and Hair," *NWSA Journal* 18, no. 2 (Summer 2006): 24–51.

10. Nicholas Parco, "Ivy League Prof Profiled on Plane, Questioned over Math Equation," *Daily News* (May 7, 2016), accessed May 10, 2016, http://www.nydailynews.com/news/national/ivy -league-prof-profiled-plane-questioned-math-equation-article -1.2628542.

11. Shanell T. Smith, *The Woman Babylon and the Marks of Empire: Reading Revelation with a Postcolonial Womanist Hermeneutics of Ambiveilence* (Minneapolis: Fortress, 2014), 154–74.

Chapter 6: Spirit

1. *Baptism, Eucharist, and Ministry* (Geneva: World Council of Churches, 1982), §"Baptism," para. 5.

2. Presbyterian *Book of Common Worship* (Louisville, KY: Westminster/John Knox Press, 1993), 413.

3. *The Compact Edition of the Oxford English Dictionary*, s.v. "improve" (Oxford: Oxford University Press, 1971).

4. Presbyterian Church (U.S.A.) *Book of Confessions* (Louisville, KY: Office of the General Assembly, 2014), 7.277.

5. Ibid.

6. Presbyterian readers may notice a subtle parallel with the familiar ordination vow: to serve with "energy, intelligence, imagination, and love"; see the Presbyterian Church (U.S.A.) *Book of Order* (Louisville, KY: Office of the General Assembly, 2015–2017), W-4.4003 h. This is fitting, as ordination flows from baptism: each Christian's call to ministry in Jesus' name.

7. See Dorothy C. Bass, ed. *Practicing Our Faith: A Way of Life for*

a Searching People (San Francisco: Jossey-Bass Publishers, 1997); Adele Ahlberg Calhoun, *Spiritual Disciplines Handbook: Practices That Transform Us* (Downers Grove, IL: InterVarsity Press, 2005); Richard J. Foster, *Celebration of Discipline: The Path to Spiritual Growth, Revised Edition* (San Francisco: HarperSanFrancisco, 1988); Christine D. Pohl, *Living into Community: Cultivating Practices That Sustain Us* (Grand Rapids: Eedrmans Publishing Company, 2012); Marjorie J. Thompson, *Soul Feast: An Invitation to the Christian Spiritual Life* (Louisville, KY: Westminster John Knox Press, 2014).

8. Presbyterian Church (U.S.A.) *Book of Confessions* (Louisville, KY: Office of the General Assembly, 2014), 7.001.

Chapter 7: Body

1. Michael Pollan, *In Defense of Food: An Eater's Manifesto* (New York: Penguin Press, 2009), 1.

2. Erin Walsh, "From Online Safety to Digital Citizenship: Parenting in an Online World," Mind Positive Parenting, http://drdavewalsh.com/speaking/topics#onlinesafety.

3. Kris Tostengard Michel, "What Are You Worth: Proverbs 22:9" (unpublished sermon, Bethlehem Lutheran Church, October 4, 2015).

4. James B. Nelson, *Embodiment: An Approach to Sexuality and Christian Theology* (Minneapolis: Augsburg Publishing House, 1978), 47–58.

5. Pierre Bourdieu, *Pascalian Meditations*, trans. Richard Nice (Stanford: Stanford University Press, 2000).

Chapter 8: Community

1. Rob Bell made good use of this insight in his two *Everything Is Spiritual* speaking tours, the first of which (2006) is available on DVD and the second of which (2016) is available for free at http://robbell.com. He writes about these ideas in *What We Talk about When We Talk about God* (New York: HarperOne, 2013), 21–80. See also Ernest L. Simmons, *The Entangled Trinity: Quantum Physics and Theology* (Minneapolis: Fortress Press, 2014).

2. Greg Garrison, "Futuristic Church with 12-Lane Bowling Alley, 7 Giant Domes and an Observation Tower Opens Its Doors to the Public," Alabama Media Group (July 16, 2014), accessed April 12, 2016, http://www.al.com/living/index.ssf/2014/07/futuristic_church_with_12-lane.html.

3. Robert D. Putnam, *Bowling Alone: The Collapse and Revival of American Community* (New York: Simon & Schuster, 2000). Putnam's book-length treatment is based on an essay published in 1995.

4. Ibid., 19.

5. Robert Wuthnow, *Loose Connections: Joining Together in America's*

Fragmented Communities (Cambridge: Harvard University Press, 1998).

6. Lee Rainie and Barry Wellman, *Networked: The New Social Operating System* (Cambridge: MIT Press, 2012), 12.

7. Marc J. Dunkelman, *The Vanishing Neighbor: The Transformation of American Community* (New York: W. W. Norton & Company, 2014).

8. Ibid., 100.

9. Jonathan R. Wilson, *Living Faithfully in a Fragmented World: From Macintyre's After Virtue to a New Monasticism*, 2nd ed., New Monastic Library 6 (Eugene, OR: Cascade Books, 2010).

10. Paul Sparks, Tim Sorens, and Dwight J. Friesen, *The New Parish: How Neighborhood Churches Are Transforming Mission, Discipleship and Community* (Downers Grove: IVP Books, 2014).

11. Mark Lau Branson and Nicholas Warnes, eds., *Starting Missional Churches: Life with God in the Neighborhood* (Downers Grove: IVP Books, 2014).

12. Reggie McNeal, *Missional Communities: The Rise of the Post-Congregational Church* (San Francisco: Jossey-Bass, 2011).

13. For examples of the former, see East End Fellowship in Richmond, VA, and Church of the Savior in Washington, DC. For examples of the latter, see Kelly Bean, *How to Be a Christian without Going to Church: The Unofficial Guide to Alternative Forms of Christian Community* (Grand Rapids: Baker Books, 2014).

14. Jay Pathak and Dave Runyon, *The Art of Neighboring: Building Genuine Relationships Right outside Your Door* (Grand Rapids: Baker Books, 2012).

15. C. Christopher Smith, *Slow Church: Cultivating Community in the Patient Way of Jesus* (Downers Grove: IVP Books, 2014).

16. Alexia Salvatierra, *Faith-Rooted Organizing: Mobilizing the Church in Service to the World* (Downers Grove: IVP Books, 2014).

17. Dunkelman, *The Vanishing Neighbor*, 235.

18. http://sweatysheep.com.

19. http://sweatysheep.com/discover/what-is-sweaty-sheep/.

20. Paul Adams, *Grouped: How Small Groups of Friends Are the Key to Influence on the Social Web* (Berkeley: New Riders, 2012), 36–40.

21. Rainie and Wellman note that it is cognitively easier to think we belong to groups instead of social networks. See *Networked*, 35.

22. On clusters and foci in social networks, see ibid., 51–54.

23. For an excellent example of a hybrid approach see Keith Anderson's metaphor of "in cathedral" in *The Digital Cathedral: Networked Ministry in a Wireless World* (New York: Morehouse Publishing, 2015).

Chapter 9: Work

1. See the Collegeville Institute Seminars at http://collegevilleinstitute .org/the-seminars/, accessed March 31, 2016. In addition to several book projects, the Seminars have created two small-group resources: *Called to Life*, accessed August 5, 2015, www.called-to-life.com, and *Called to Work*, accessed August 5, 2015, www.called-to-work.com. We have listened to hundreds of people in Protestant and Catholic congregations share stories of God's callings in their lives and have conducted interviews with more than thirty professionals. Some of these interviews are available through our video narrative project, *Lives Explored*, accessed December 6, 2015, http://www.lives -explored.com/; one story is Denise's, which is used by permission.

2. International Janitorial Cleaning Services, accessed March 23, 2016, http://www.ijcsa.org/About/International-Janitorial-Cleaning -Services-Association.

3. I have changed the names of the people interviewed unless otherwise indicated.

4. See the stories of Francois and Lauren at http://www.lives-explored .com/, accessed March 31, 2016.

5. J. Stuart Bunderson and Jeffery A. Thompson, "The Call of the Wild: Zookeepers, Callings, and the Double-edged Sword of Deeply Meaningful Work," *Administrative Science Quarterly* 54 (2009): 32–57, at 36.

6. See John Neafsey, *Act Justly, Love Tenderly: Lifelong Lessons on Calling and Conscience* (Maryknoll, NY: Orbis, 2016).

7. See Michael Himes, "Working to Answer Three Key Questions," *Visitation Monastery of Minneapolis* (February 4, 2010), accessed December 6, 2015, http://www.visitationmonasteryminneapolis .org/2010/02/on-discernment-three-key-questions/.

Chapter 10: Mind

1. *The Constitution of the Presbyterian Church (U.S.A.)*, Part I, *Book of Confessions* (Louisville, KY: Office of the General Assembly, Presbyterian Church (U.S.A.), 2014), 4.001.

2. Brian A. Gerrish, *The Eucharistic Theology of John Calvin* (Minneapolis: Fortress Press, 1993), 179.

3. For an excellent exposition of this, see Mark Labberton, *Called: The Crisis and Promise of Following Jesus Today* (Downers Grove, IL: InterVarsity Press, 2014). See also his two prior volumes on worship and justice: *The Dangerous Act of Worship: Living God's Call to Justice* (Downers Grove, IL: InterVarsity Press, 2012) and *The Dangerous Act of Loving Your Neighbor: Seeing Others through the Eyes of Jesus* (Downers Grove, IL: InterVarsity Press, 2010).

4. See *Liturgical-Missional: Perspectives on a Reformed Ecclesiology*,

ed. Neal D. Presa; foreword by Olav Fykse Tveit (Eugene, OR: Pick-wick Publications/Wipf and Stock, 2016). This recent volume includes many insightful essays on the mutual relationship of worship and mission, putting into necessary conversation liturgical theology and missional theology, exploring issues related to the gathered/sent community, or the people of God as worshiping/witnessing communities.

5. See Michael Horton, *Introducing Covenant Theology* (Grand Rapids, MI: Baker Books, 2009), on his excellent exposition of absence in presence and presence in absence and his subsequent volumes in that series on covenant.

6. One of the few expositions of Barth's theology of the ascension is Andrew Burgess, *The Ascension in Karl Barth* (Aldershot: Ashgate, 2004).

7. Sang Hyun Lee, *From a Liminal Place: An Asian American Theology* (Minneapolis: Fortress Press, 2010).

Contributors

Margaret P. Aymer is associate professor of New Testament at Austin Presbyterian Theological Seminary. She is the author of *James: Diaspora Rhetorics of a Friend of God* (Sheffield Phoenix, 2015) and *First Pure, Then Peaceable: Frederick Douglass, Darkness, and the Epistle of James* (T&T Clark, 2007). She has also co-edited and written articles for *Fortress Commentary on the New Testament* (Fortress, 2014) and *Islanders, Islands, and the Bible: Ruminations* (SBL, 2015). In addition to these, she is the author of many articles and short commentaries, including her entry on "Acts of the Apostles" for the *Women's Bible Commentary* (WJK, 2012). She is an ordained teaching elder in the Presbyterian Church (U.S.A.), and her Bible study "Confessing the Beatitudes" has been commended to the church for study. Margaret shares her life with her beloved husband, Laurent Oget, and their son, Gabriel. (See chap. 5: Privilege/Incarnation.)

Kathleen A. Cahalan is professor of practical theology at Saint John's University School of Theology and Seminary, Collegeville, MN. Cahalan leads a collaborative, ecumenical, and interdisciplinary research project at the Collegeville Institute, exploring vocation in relationship to the professions, across the lifespan, and through interfaith perspectives. She is the author of books for a broad church audience, including *Living Your*

Discipleship: Seven Ways to Express Your Deepest Calling, co-authored with Laura Kelly Fanucci (Twenty-Third, 2015), and *The Stories We Live: Finding God's Calling All around Us* (Eerdmans, 2017); scholarly books on vocation include *Calling in Today's World: Voices from Eight Faith Perspectives,* edited with Douglas J. Schuurman (Eerdmans, 2017), and *Calling All Years Good: Vocation across the Lifespan,* edited with Bonnie Miller-McLemore (Eerdmans, 2017). (See chap. 9: Work.)

Adam J. Copeland is director of Stewardship Leadership at Luther Seminary in St. Paul, MN, where he teaches as well as directs the Center for Stewardship Leaders. He is editor of *Kissing in the Chapel, Praying in the Frat House: Wrestling with Faith and College* (Rowman & Littlefield, 2014). Having served as a rural pastor, church planter, and college professor, his scholarly interests now include stewardship and generosity, church leadership, rhetoric, and digital culture. His articles have appeared in the *Christian Century, Journal for Preachers, Hybrid Pedagogy,* the *Journal of Religion and Popular Culture,* and in more than ten books. He holds degrees from St. Olaf College and Columbia Theological Seminary, and is a Ph.D. candidate in rhetoric, writing, and culture at North Dakota State University. Find him online at http://adamjcopeland.com. (See chap. 4: Technology.)

MaryAnn McKibben Dana is a writer, pastor, and speaker living in the Virginia suburbs of Washington, DC. She is author of *Sabbath in the Suburbs: A Family's Experiment with Holy Time* (Chalice Press, 2012) and *Improvising with God* (Eerdmans, 2017). Her writing has appeared in *TIME.com,* the *Washington Post, Religion Dispatches, Journal for Preachers,* and the *Christian Century.* She has been featured on PBS's *Religion and Ethics Newsweekly* for her work on Sabbath and was recognized by the Presbyterian Writers Guild with the 2015–2016 David Steele Distinguished Writer Award. She is a mother of three, a haphazard knitter, and an occasional marathoner. Connect with her at her website, The Blue Room (http://theblueroomblog.org). (See chap. 1: Time.)

David Gambrell has been an associate for worship in the Presbyterian Church (U.S.A.) Office of Theology and Worship since 2007. In that capacity he has served as an ex officio member of the Presbyterian Committee on Congregational Song (responsible for the 2013 hymnal *Glory to God*), a representative to the Consultation on Common Texts (responsible for the *Revised Common Lectionary*), and coordinated a revision to the PC(USA) *Directory for Worship*, part of the denomination's *Book of Order*. David is editor of the quarterly journal *Call to Worship* and co-editor, with Kimberly Bracken Long, of a forthcoming revision to the Presbyterian *Book of Common Worship* (WJKP, 2018). He was a contributor to the six-volume *Feasting on the Word Worship Companion* series and a collection of *Inclusive Marriage Services* (WJKP, 2015). He is also the author of a collection of hymn texts titled *Breathing Spirit into Dust* (GIA, 2015). He has an M.Div. from Austin Presbyterian Theological Seminary and the Ph.D. in liturgical studies from Garrett-Evangelical Theological Seminary. (See chap. 6: Spirit.)

David P. King is the Karen Lake Buttrey Director of the Lake Institute on Faith and Giving as well as assistant professor of philanthropic studies within the Indiana University Lilly Family School of Philanthropy. He arrived at IUPUI in 2014, after serving as assistant professor of Christian History at Memphis Theological Seminary in Memphis, TN. He earned a master of divinity degree from Duke Divinity School and completed a Ph.D. in religion from Emory University in 2012. Having served local churches and national faith-based organizations as an ordained Baptist minister, he is also fueled by facilitating conversations with faith leaders, donors, and fundraisers (of all generations) on the intersections of faith and giving. Trained as an American religious historian, his research interests include investigating how the religious identity of faith-based nonprofits shapes their motivations, rhetoric, and practice. (See chap. 3: Money and Finances.)

Neal D. Presa is associate pastor of Village Community Presbyterian Church in Rancho Santa Fe, CA, and adjunct assistant professor of worship at Fuller Theological Seminary and was Extraordinary Associate Professor of Practical Theology of the North-West University in Potchefstroom, South Africa. In

2012, he was elected moderator of the 220th General Assembly of the Presbyterian Church (U.S.A.). He served as a solo pastor in Middlesex, NJ, and on the faculty of New Brunswick Theological Seminary, where he taught worship, preaching, and Presbyterian studies. He is the author and editor of five books, including *Our Only Comfort: 52 Reflections on the Heidelberg Catechism* (WJKP, 2015) and *Liturgical-Missional: Perspectives on a Reformed Ecclesiology* (Pickwick, 2016), and has contributed essays and chapters in numerous journals and books on ecumenism, pastoral theology, preaching, and worship. He is the regular book reviewer for *The Living Pulpit*, an online journal for preachers, and has served on the editorial board of *Studia Liturgica*, the international peer-reviewed journal of *Societas Liturgica*, in which he holds membership, along with the North American Academy of Liturgy. Neal is married to Grace, and with their two sons and puppy, they live in Carlsbad, CA. (See chap. 10: Mind.)

Ellie Roscher is the director of youth and story development at Bethlehem Lutheran Church Twin Cities. Author of *Play like a Girl* (Viva Editions, 2017) and *How Coffee Saved My Life* (Chalice, 2009), she is an editor, blogger, speaker, and teacher. Ellie earned her MA in theology from Luther Seminary and her MFA in creative writing from Sarah Lawrence College. She lives in Minneapolis with her spouse and two sons, and you can find more of her work at http://ellieroscher.com. (See chap. 7: Body.)

Mary Hinkle Shore holds a Ph.D. in New Testament and christian origins from Duke University and has been an ordained Lutheran minister for thirty years. Having worked both as a parish pastor and seminary professor, she currently serves a congregation in the mountains of western North Carolina. In that context, she has been active in efforts to increase patient- and family-centered care in the Mission Health System, as well as instrumental in the founding of Mountain Neighbors Network, a collection of members and volunteers whose aim is to help elders stay socially engaged and living longer in their own homes. She reflects on stewardship and congregational practice from within academic interests that include the letters of Paul. Her current writing projects include an essay that brings Pauline thought into conversation with recent research on shame and vulnerability. (See chap. 2: Life at Its End.)

John W. Vest is the visiting assistant professor of evangelism at Union Presbyterian Seminary in Richmond, VA. Prior to this appointment, he served in congregational ministry for fifteen years in the Chicago metropolitan area, most recently as the associate pastor for youth ministry at the Fourth Presbyterian Church of Chicago. He holds degrees from Rice University, the University of Chicago Divinity School, and McCormick Theological Seminary, and has studied at the Hebrew University of Jerusalem. He is co-founder of the Progressive Youth Ministry conference and has published a collection of confirmation sermons called *It's Not Conformation* (CreateSpace, 2015). An enthusiastic pit-master, John dreams of one day achieving the mystical union of church and BBQ. Blog posts and information about his various ministry projects, including a new worshiping community in the Richmond area, can be found at http://john-vest.com. (See chap. 8: Community.)

CPSIA information can be obtained
at www.ICGtesting.com
Printed in the USA
LVOW03s2359030817
543472LV00014B/154/P